Understanding the
Afterlife
in
This Life

Bernie Kastner, Ph.D.

DEVORA
PUBLISHING
JERUSALEM ◆ NEW YORK

To Gadi,

Of blessed memory,

a pure and precious soul,

who graduated

to his eternal world

in June 2003

Acknowledgments

I would like to begin this section with heartfelt thanks to my wife, Iva, whose dedication in keeping things going in the family allowed me to be free to tackle the challenges inherent in this endeavor; to our children for allowing me to raise at the dinner table many of the topics covered in this book; and especially to our always-to-be 19-year-old son, Gedalia Natan, our special angel in whose memory I became inspired to pursue the subject of this work. Deepest thanks to my Mom, Mrs. Hedy Kastner, and to Mrs. Frances Korenblit, both of whom encouraged me in every which way to take on this project.

Special thanks to Chani Hadad and to Daniella Barak for their helpful editorial insights and organization of the text, and to Yaacov Peterseil for his foresight regarding the value this material could have within the community at large. Additional thanks go to Rabbi Chaim Richman and Dr. Oz and Orit Martin for their ongoing encouragement and support.

I would also like to thank the participants of the research group who graciously took time out of their busy schedules in order to be a part of the initial study I conducted on overcoming the fear of death.

Last but not least, I am grateful to Our Creator who put me in the position to complete this work so that others can benefit and gain from the knowledge contained herein.

Contents

Preface

My purpose in compiling the material for this book goes far beyond the academic realm. The loss of our 19-year-old son to a devastating illness brought me closer in contact with death than I had ever experienced. It forced me to take a true, hard look at what life is and what happens after we die. I began reading avidly on the subject of death and dying, the processes involved, and the coping mechanisms employed by professionals, family, and the patients themselves.

One of the first books both my wife and I read on the subject that made a huge impact on us was *Soul Searching* by Rabbi Yaakov Astor. It led me to explore what we know about the world before we are born, the world that exists in the afterlife, reincarnation, and of the many near-death experiences widely documented in scientific literature. His book brought together peer-reviewed research and a wide range of Torah sources to show the many parallels between them.

I later realized that aside from Astor's book, there are many other sources of information that are literally filled with eye-opening testimony on the meaning of our lives here in this world and what awaits us in the World to Come. It would take a person a long time to wade through all that is out there before ridding himself of those anxieties connected to death and dying that impede one's happiness. So I began to highlight and then collate noteworthy sound bites, either through reading or through stories recounted to me, into what I called "Bibliotherapy." Initially, it was my way of strengthening myself – as if I was giving myself a strong dose of *chizzuk* (encouragement) serum. As the document grew I began to share it with a group of patients and health-care professionals. The response was overwhelmingly positive.

Alas, the more I read and began to understand what it means to say goodbye to a loved one, the more I realized that the level of acceptance depends on each individual's attitude toward death. I have found that there are many people who do not know how to cope with the process of death, are downright afraid of it, and who do their utmost to block it out of their minds.

I decided that I would take a closer look at why people are afraid of death, identify those people who are unafraid or less afraid, and then try to come up with a formula toward ameliorating this fear.

I was further motivated to pursue my efforts in this specific area after reading separate statements by two well-respected professionals in the field of death and dying, both indicating that more work needs to be done to help people overcome their fear of death.

In her Preface to *On Death and Dying*, Elisabeth Kubler-Ross (xi) writes: "…encourage others not to shy away from the 'hopelessly' sick but to get closer to them, as they can help them much during their final hours. The few who can do this will also discover that it can be a mutually gratifying experience; they will learn much about the functioning of the human mind, the unique human aspects of our existence, and will emerge from the experience enriched and perhaps with fewer anxieties about their own finality."

The last few words "and perhaps with fewer anxieties about their own finality" bespeaks the need to be more definitive in helping people reduce this anxiety. What chance is there for those who cannot or will not, for whatever reason, attempt to get closer to a person on his or her deathbed, to overcome their own fears and anxieties about death? And for those who do, this seems to be the tip of the iceberg. Why wait until we come in contact with a dying patient? Why wait until it is forced upon us suddenly? Why not initiate therapy and do some prevention?

Dr. Rachel Naomi Remen, whose work with extremely ill and dying patients is widely known, suggests, "Perhaps we need more sensitive tools for studying emotional and psychological states. The sensitivity of our emotional assessment needs to equal the sophistication of our immunological knowledge, and we are not there yet."

A life free of the fear of death is a great blessing. Since most people would agree with that, it's rather strange how little we are currently doing to learn whether that blessing can be spread more widely.

It may be true that those who cling to religion and have a deeper appreciation for life after life will probably have a better attitude toward death and dying. But this is the kind of subject matter that isn't taught in school, and therefore even those exposed to religion may come up short on the fear-of-death scale.

Mark A.R. Kleiman, in an article entitled "Overcoming the fear of death," states that not to fear death is a gift. It doesn't imply carelessness about life; one might have excellent reasons for wanting to stay alive. However, life becomes sweeter by not having to be burdened by the horror of dying.

So what, if anything, could confer that gift? Psychologists have learned how to measure the fear of death, but not to change it. Those who have entered mystical states or undergone near death experiences (NDES) frequently report that they have lost their fear of dying.[1] So is it possible to substitute an acute event such as an NDE with another intervention, such as a powerful movie, thus creating the same result (that is, a decrease in the fear of death)?

One who genuinely comes to view our current existence in a larger perspective weathers life's frustrations more easily and revels in its triumphs more intensely than those who do not attain that same high ground (Astor 29). I believe that the best time to overcome the fear of death is before it comes knocking at your front door. Each individual must decide for himself when he is ready to face this issue head on. It may not be too early, though, to introduce the subject even to someone in their 20s, when they are just beginning to venture into their adulthood.

Dr. Lewis Thomas, past President of Memorial Sloan-Kettering Cancer Center in New York, summed up this point:

There are some odd things about human dying, anyway, that don't fit at all with the notion of agony at the end. People who almost die but don't, and then recover to describe the experience, never mention anguish or pain, or even despair; to the contrary they recall a strange, unfamiliar feeling of tranquility and peace. The act of dying seems to be associated with some other event, perhaps pharmacologic, that transforms it into something quite different from what most of us are brought up to anticipate...Something is probably going on that we don't yet know about.

And finally, I'd like to bring one other piece of reinforcement for delving into the topic of this book. Dr. Sukie Miller, a psychotherapist and one of the first researchers to study the cross-cultural

---

1.   That's one of the questions involving the use of ergot (Kerenyi, 1967). Aged barley, and many other grains, may contain the fungus ergot which contains LSA, a precursor to LSD. It is possible that users were hallucinating and very open to suggestion; hence the possibility that they were ready to imagine having seen the secrets of life after death and believe in them totally. This theory, however, remains controversial.

dimensions of the afterdeath, and author of *After Death – Mapping the Journey*, said that extensive literature searches have revealed a distinct scarcity of studies designed to prove that exposure to ideas and images of the afterdeath actually brings benefits to the seeker.

For the reader's edification, the central focus of the book lies in its bibliotherapy – a compilation of short vignettes culled from many different sources. Bibliotherapy acts as a repository of invaluable information for an individual who does not have the time or the will to begin a massive search for answers to questions that have gnawed at him for years. It is heavy-hitting and direct – essentially providing a foundation that one may need in order to begin the journey toward drastically reducing or obliterating his fear of death. The other two sections are designed to provide evidence and specific background information thus giving the reader a richer perspective. Some of the contents in Part One is expanded upon in the Selected Literature Review Section at the end of the book.

As I mentioned earlier, the reader need not begin his search for answers by painstakingly reading 50 or more books on the subject. I have attempted to bring together in one source over 140 of these "gems." (I am sure there are many more, but at the time of this printing I had to draw the line somewhere.) They are designed so that each reader can examine for himself to what extent the various reference material presented here positively affects his outlook on life in this world and on life in the World to Come. I welcome additional stories and sources that are aimed at strengthening one's outlook in the face of a life-threatening illness or in helping one navigate the grieving process following the death of a loved one.

It is my hope that upon finishing this book you take with you the following: a renewed sense of appreciation and gratefulness for our lives here in this world; a better understanding of what awaits us in the next world; and a decrease in your anxiety level vis-à-vis death and dying.

PART ONE

Seeing Behind the Curtain

Introduction

What We Know About
Life after Death

hree buddies die in a car accident and go to heaven for an orientation. They are all asked, "When you are lying there at your funeral and friends and family are mourning over you, what would you like to hear them say about you?" The first guy says, "I would like to hear them say that I was a great doctor of my time, and a great family man." The second guy says, "I would like to hear that I was a wonderful husband and school teacher who made a huge difference in our children of tomorrow." The last guy replies, "I would like to hear them say, 'LOOK, HE'S MOVING!!!!!'

Even in the context of this joke, we see that there are those who deny death and will do everything in their power to avoid thinking about what there may be in the beyond.

The Gesher HaChaim, Rabbi Yechiel Michel Tucazinsky, once said that just as the life of an embryo merely constitutes the transition to a broader and more exciting life, so, to an even greater extent, is life on Earth merely the prelude to a more fascinating, glorious life, which man, confined within his physical body and with limited perception, is incapable of conceiving.

Dr. Irvin Yalom, a noted psychiatrist, wrote:

> We humans go through life in stages. As very young children, we think about death a great deal; some of us even obsess about it…And before long, we realize that death will come to everyone – to our grandma, to our mother and father, even to ourselves. We brood about this in private. Our parents and teachers, thinking it's bad for children to think about death, either keep silent about it or give us fairy tales about a heaven and angels, eternal reunion, reincarnation, immortal souls. So we push it out of our minds, or we openly defy death…I for one, picture my life as a brilliant spark between two vast and identical pools of darkness: the darkness existing before my birth and the darkness following my death. Isn't it astounding how much we dread the latter darkness and how indifferent we are to the first?

Secular literature and our own Judaic sources are filled with information regarding the afterlife, but few of us take notice. Our prayers contain many references to the World to Come, but how many of us can truly say that we know what it's like over there? Death and dying surrounds us – whether it happens naturally or by an accident or act of terror – and most of us relate to the incident from the point of view of how *we*, those who are left behind, feel. Why not consider where the person who passed on went to? Instead of making ourselves or the family members the subject of our emotions, how about taking another leap forward to try and understand what it may be like for the one who crossed over into the life after this one? What is he or she doing now? Are they doing the same kinds of things they did here just in a different place? Are they now angels? Is there a *bet midrash* where they could sit with their *chavrutot* and learn? Do they get to meet our great leaders and *rabbanim* of yesteryear? Can we ask Moshe

Rabbeinu what it was like for him to lead the Jewish people? Are there really baseball games up in heaven?[2]

Human beings are burdened with the cognitive capacity to be aware of their own inevitable mortality and to fear what may come afterwards. This creates an existential fear of death – the fear of not existing, which is very hard to conquer. So what are the most common fears of death?

1. The finality of death – that there is no reversal, no remedy, no tomorrow.
2. The uncertainty of what follows – we all know that the fear of the unknown can be downright terrifying.
3. Annihilation anxiety or fear of non-existence – the concept of non-being can be very threatening because it goes against our strong will to continue on living forever.
4. The ultimate loss – upon death, we are forced to lose everything we have ever valued. Those with the strongest attachments towards material things are likely to fear death the most. Loss of control and of the ability to care for dependents also fall into this category.
5. Fear of the pain and loneliness in dying – many are afraid they will die alone or in pain without any family or friends around them.
6. Fear of failing to complete life work – many people are afraid of a meaningless existence than death itself; their fear stems from not being able to complete their mission or calling in life. I would add that a good majority of us go through life not knowing what we really want, not knowing what our true purpose is in this life, and hence not accomplishing that which God wanted us to achieve in this lifetime.

---

2. This reminds me of the story of an angel who comes down to earth and approaches an avid baseball fan and says to him: *I have good news and bad news for you.* What's the good news? *There are baseball double-headers every day in heaven.* Oh yeah, wow, that's great! So what could possibly be the bad news? *You're scheduled to pitch tomorrow night!*

We have a number of coping mechanisms to respond to these anxieties. Dr. Elisabeth Kubler-Ross wrote about five stages: denial, anger, bargaining, depression, and acceptance. Other methods are terror management, in which we spend a great deal of time managing our subconscious terror; living vicariously through our children or grandchildren; being religious and spiritual; the power of prayer; being creative, thus leaving something behind by which to be remembered; being philanthropical; and cultural, meaning that we identify with an institution or tradition which transcends our own death.

Death acceptance is another coping mechanism in which there is a willingness to let go by doing a life review and bringing closure to what you've accomplished, the realization that your life had meaning, that you made a difference, and by discovering who you really are, connecting to that inner sense – in effect, to your *neshama* (soul).

Despite some of the scientific evidence you'll read that suggests that consciousness survives the death of the body, many argue that life after death cannot be considered proven beyond a reasonable doubt according to strict scientific standards. If that is the case, are we being irrational if we still believe that we will have a life after death? Why should we believe in something until there is enough evidence to prove it?

Dr. Gary Doore, a scholar of contemporary philosophy and religion, responds to this by arguing that we are still acting rationally for the purpose of testing that belief in our lives – just as a scientist, with considerable determination and in the face of negative evidence or personal doubt, will adhere to a favorite theory while testing it in the laboratory. He concludes:

> …if believing makes us stronger, more courageous, more enduring for difficulties and setbacks, less prone to defeat and despair than would be the case if we adopted either agnosticism or materialism – then these are legitimate grounds for choosing to hold the belief as a working hypothesis…without

such a preliminary trust, we wouldn't have the incentive and energy to undertake the spiritual discipline necessary to verify the soul's immortality in a personally convincing way (Doore 279).

We can choose to face death with fear or with hope. We can embrace life or merely prepare ourselves to die. The question remains: How can we embrace life *and* at the same time block out our anxieties about what's going to happen to us when our time is up? I propose to you that by becoming more knowledgeable about the afterlife, this will begin the process of healing that many of us desperately seek in order to reduce our fear of death. Our increased awareness can throw a different perspective on life and move us to rearrange our priorities.

Near-Death Experiences

It would be presumptuous of me to tell you with absolute certainty what it is really like after we leave this world. So where did all this body of knowledge come from that causes people to believe that hey, maybe there really is something out there beyond what we know in this life? Well, one source of information comes from people who actually experienced dying and then minutes later were resuscitated. They remembered something happening to them during those critical moments while their lives were hanging in the balance. This phenomenon, known as an NDE, or near-death experience, is quite widespread. Throughout the world, millions of people have had this experience. It is conceivable that there are people reading this who either had an NDE themselves or know somebody who had one. Actually, many of those who have had an NDE usually suppress it out of fear of rejection or ridicule.

In 1975, Dr. Raymond Moody, a physician and philosopher, wrote a watershed book called *Life After Life*, in which he interviewed more than 1,000 people who experienced an NDE. He found some amazing facts. These people weren't just having a dream. The proof was in the similarity and accuracy of the accounts described by each of the NDEers. For example:

A man is dying and, as he reaches the point of greatest physical distress, he hears himself pronounced dead by his doctor. He begins to hear an uncomfortable noise, a loud ringing or buzzing, and at the same time feels himself moving very rapidly through a long tunnel. After this, he suddenly finds himself outside of his own physical body, but still in the immediate physical environment, and he sees his own body from a distance, as though he is a spectator. He watches the resuscitation attempt from this unusual vantage point and is in a state of emotional upheaval. After a while, he collects himself and becomes more accustomed to his odd condition. He notices that he still has a "body," but one of a very different nature and with very different powers from the physical body he has left behind. Soon other things begin to happen. Others come to meet and to help him. He glimpses the spirits of relatives and friends who have already died, and a loving, warm spirit of a kind he has never encountered before – a being of light – appears before him. This being asks him a question, non-verbally, to make him evaluate his life and helps him along by showing him a panoramic, instantaneous playback of the major events of his life. At some point he finds himself approaching some sort of barrier or border, apparently representing the limit between earthly life and the next life. Yet, he finds that he must go back to earth, that the time for his death has not yet come. At this point he resists, for by now he is taken up with his experiences in the afterlife and does not want to return. He is overwhelmed by intense feelings of joy, love, and peace. He realizes that love and knowledge are two of the most important things that there are. Despite his attitude, though, he somehow reunites with his physical body and lives. Later he tries to tell others, but he has trouble doing so. In the first place, he can find no human words adequate to describe these unearthly episodes. He also finds that others scoff, so he stops telling other people. Still, the experience affects his life profoundly, especially his views about death and its relationship to life.

Dr. Michael Sabom, a cardiologist at the Atlanta VA Medical Center, devoted a chapter in his book *Recollections of Death* to the implications of the near-death experience on the survivor and on the medical community at large. He writes: "What I have observed convinces me that the NDE is a truly significant event for both the patient and his physician. Moreover, the psychological impact of this experience at the point of near-death may play a role in the physical outcome of the resuscitation itself by affecting a powerful but poorly understood aspect of human life – the will to live" (124).

He reports that death anxiety was dramatically reduced, if not totally eliminated, by the NDEer. Individuals surviving similar types of near-death crisis events without associated NDEs, however, did not evidence this change in death fears. Furthermore, this reduction in death anxiety was readily evident not only at the time of the initial interview but also months or years later. Associated with this decrease in death anxiety was the strong personal conviction that the NDE represented a privileged glimpse of what was to occur at the moment of final bodily death. In one case followed by Sabom, a patient said many times before experiencing an NDE, "I don't want to die, I'm too young to die"; after it he said, "Well, I'm going to do the best I can, and when my time comes, I'm ready for it" (125).

Hypnotherapy/Guided Imagery

It has been shown that highly specific imagery can bring about changes in the body. In one such study of many, Dr. Howard Hall of Pennsylvania State University has shown that subjects, using hypnosis, can generate a more active immune response when they imagine their white blood cells as "strong and powerful sharks"

(Locke & Colligen). Working with 126 cancer patients, psycho-physiologist Jeanne Achterberg and psychologist G. Frank Lawlis demonstrated that the patients' clinical response – future growth or remission – was directly related to the specificity, vividness, strength, and clarity of their mental imagery.

The usefulness of visualization (hypnotherapy, guided imagery) in treating cancer has also been well researched. (O.C. Simonton, S. Simonton, & Creighton) There is strong evidence that some cancer patients live longer and/or go into remission if they regularly and vividly visualize their bodies attacking diseased cells. Both children and adults can use these techniques. Likewise, emotional states also have a powerful effect on our physical well-being. When Norman Cousins was diagnosed with an "incurable" collagen disease, he discovered that laughter helps improve some people's immune systems. He conquered his disease by watching funny movies every day. Laughing for thirty to sixty minutes a day seems to be good medicine. It reduces people's pain and helps them heal.

Two years ago I conducted a research study to see if it were possible to help people overcome their fear of death by exposing them to images and ideas of what we know about the afterlife. A four-part counseling intervention was administered to an experimental group designed to measure whether their current anxiety towards death and dying could be significantly decreased. Questionnaires were used in order to capture these attitudes immediately before and after the intervention and at three months after the intervention. A control group was also set up for comparative purposes. Sixty-eight percent of the participants showed a decrease in their death anxiety immediately after the intervention. Overall death anxiety scores decreased by 6.8%; at the three-month mark, this figure was 6.2%, both figures statistically significant. Watching a video on the topic and a bibliotherapy session using a customized document containing selected material were reported to be the more effective interventional modules in reducing death anxiety (guided imagery and a personal account by an NDEer were the other two interventions). The trend among the study group seems to have resulted in a positive attitudinal change in how they now conduct themselves in their current lives and in coping with what awaits them on the "other side." Interestingly, in corresponding handwriting samples I studied, there is evidence of graphic changes that reflect the newly manifested attitudes borne out from the research intervention. However, more empirical evidence is needed in order to make wider, sweeping statements regarding the probability of success utilizing these methods in either a group or in a one to one counseling setting.

The Afterlife

In perhaps what many arguably consider to be the most important piece of scientific literature published within the last few years on the subject of near-death experiences, we may begin to find some answers to the notion about the afterlife. In the December 15, 2001, issue of *The Lancet*, an article entitled, "Near-death experience in survivors of cardiac arrest: a prospective study in the Netherlands" aimed to establish the cause of near-death experiences after a life-threatening crisis, and to assess factors that affected its frequency, depth, and content (van Lommel, van Wees, Meyers, & Elfferich).

The *Lancet* authors conclude, "the thus far assumed, but never proven, concept that consciousness and memories are localized in the brain should be discussed. How could a clear consciousness outside of one's body be experienced at the moment that the brain no longer functions during a period of clinical death with [a] flat EEG?...NDES push at the limits of medical ideas about the range of human consciousness and the mind-brain relation."

In a related study publicized via a February 16, 2001, news release by the University of Southampton (United Kingdom), researchers published a paper in the February issue of the medical journal *Resuscitation* detailing their pioneering study into near death experiences that suggests consciousness and the mind may continue to exist after the brain has ceased to function and the body is clinically dead.

The team spent a year studying people resuscitated in the city's General Hospital after suffering a heart attack. The patients brought back to life were all, for varying lengths of time, clinically dead with no pulse, no respiration and fixed dilated pupils. Independent EEG studies have confirmed that the brain's electrical activity, and hence brain function, ceases at that time. But seven out of 63 (11 per cent) of the Southampton patients who survived their cardiac arrest recalled emotions and visions during unconsciousness. They recalled feelings of peace and joy, time speeded up, heightened senses, lost awareness of body, seeing a bright light, entering another world, encountering a mystical being or deceased relative and coming to a point of no return.

This raises the question of how such lucid thought processes can occur when the brain is dead. Dr. Sam Parnia, a Southampton University clinical research fellow said: "The main significance of the NDE lies in the understanding of the relationship between mind and brain which has remained a topic of debate in contemporary philosophy, psychology and neuroscience." Very little is known scientifically about the subjective experience of dying, the nature of the human mind and its outcome during 'clinical death.' This is becoming a very important issue in medicine.

Skeptics came up with three explanations for these accounts, and each one was refuted by the study. The first is physiological; that the hallucinations patients experience is due to disturbed brain chemistry caused by drug treatment, a lack of oxygen or changes in carbon dioxide levels. In the Southampton study none of the four patients who had NDEs had low levels of oxygen or received any unusual combination of drugs during their resuscitation.

A second explanation is that out of body experiences and vivid encounters with tunnels, lights or deceased relatives are constructed by the mind to ease the process of death. Dr. Parnia added: "The features of the NDES in this study were dissimilar to those of confusional hallucinations as they were highly structured, narrative, easily recalled and clear...During cardiac arrest brainstem activity is rapidly lost. It should not be able to sustain such lucid processes or allow the formation of lasting memories."

The third explanation is transcendental, an event indicating the continuation of life after death. All four Southampton study patients who reported an NDE were Christians but none described themselves as practicing, nor did they see religious figures during their experience.

The World To Come

One of the basic assumptions in successfully overcoming fear of death is being convinced that there was a "before" and there will be an "after". The Zohar (1:186b) states, "as long as a person is unsuccessful in his purpose in this world, the Holy One, blessed be He, uproots him and replants him over and over again." Another way of looking at this is that a person needs to fix one small trait, and needs only a short period of time in this world in order to accomplish that objective before returning to the World to Come. This can possibly explain why a baby of three months dies, or why an otherwise young adult may pass on before (what our society considers to be) his time. Using the same line of reasoning, The Ramban (Nachmanides), in his commentary to the book of *Iyov* (Job), explains that reincarnation can help shed light on why good things happen to bad people and why bad things happen to good people.

The primary source in the Torah for reincarnation is found in *Kohelet*, (Ecclesiastes) 1:4:

One generation passeth away and another generation cometh and the earth abideth forever.

The *Zohar Chadash* (chap. 33a) tells us that what this verse really means is that the generation that has passed away is the same generation that comes to replace it. Dr. Philip Berg points out that an identical key may be found in the Ten Commandments (Exodus 20:5), which says, "The sins of the fathers are remembered even unto the third and fourth generation." This does not imply, as some erroneously have contended, that God is so full of wrath that He is not content to punish merely the sinner, but that He will inflict punishment for sin upon the sinner's innocent grandchildren and great-grandchildren as well. Who could rationally love and worship so fierce and vengeful a deity? The Zohar reveals that the truth of that verse is that the third and fourth generations are, in fact, the first – one soul returning in the form of its own descendents so that it may correct the sins cited as "sins of the fathers." Such examples in support of the case of reincarnation abound in the Torah. Belief in reincarnation is another basic building block necessary to have in order to develop a mechanism to overcome the fear of death and dying.

Some rationalize: If one has no fear of falling asleep and waking up the next morning, then why be afraid of the moment of dying? "One moment you're conscious, and at the next instant you're asleep. There's literally nothing to it." Think about it.

When new attitudes regarding death and the hereafter were integrated into the lives of individuals, a new fervor for day-to-day living was often apparent. For the terminally ill or dying, the effect was usually to focus attention on living for the here and now and away from a preoccupation with death and fear of the unknown. This resulted in a renewed will to live. Another patient of Sabom's said: "I know where I'm headed to, so that I don't have to worry about dying anymore.... I've been through death and it don't bother me. I'm not scared of it. Death is nothing to go through anymore. It's not that hard to die.... I know where I'm headed to and I've got my life to live. I enjoy it a lot more."

Sabom's research is useful in that it reinforces the notion

that sharing the experiences of his patients with those who are anxiety-ridden can possibly help soften their fears. In yet another research study conducted by him, not only did medically ignorant NDE patients give significantly more accurate accounts of the efforts to save their lives than the control group (cardiac patients who did not have NDEs but were asked to describe their ordeals), but the NDE patients could do things like accurately describe the readings on machines not in their "line of sight even if their eyes had been open." This is an amazing phenomenon, and an example of the type of description of a real event that can positively affect someone who believes that death is the absolute end.

Those who try to refute NDEs claim that there are other theories that could explain this phenomenon, such as: expectation, administered drugs, endorphins, oxygen depletion, excess carbon dioxide, temporal lobe stimulation. Each of these theories, however, does not hold up. For example, many classic cases have been reported by drug-free patients and by people who were falling from mountains or involved in other accidents in which no drugs were involved. Although expectation may change the details of NDEs, it cannot be used to explain their occurrence entirely or even to account for the similarities across ages and cultures. The effects of anoxia, or lack of oxygen, are not like those of NDEs for the simple reason mentioned earlier that anoxia produces confusion rather than the clear thinking of a typical NDE.

Many theorists argue that something beyond the brain is involved – for example, that there is a soul that leaves the body at death and that the NDE is a glimpse of what follows. The Zohar provides us with proof of this:

Right before the moment of passing to the next world, as the soul gets ready to leave the body, the soul is given permission to see an overall perspective from above, just as it was given a tour of a similar perspective before entering the body before birth, and in that moment the ultimate spirit engulfs him and shows him what is to transpire in the future (his reward in the World to Come). Then God reveals himself to the soul, and out of sheer ecstasy and desire to connect with its holiness, the soul begins drawing nearer by leaving the body. This is why many times we see the eyes of the deceased remain open during the passing process because of the wonderful, glorious image he just saw. He also is in a state of calmness, satisfaction, and comfort knowing that he is being taken care of very well. Hence it is incumbent upon those who are present to close the deceased's eyes so as not to "see" something that is less noble than what he just saw (*Zohar, Vayehi*, 226:1, also *Midrash Rabba – Chaye Sarah* 62:2).

While direct evidence for this explanation is virtually impossible to obtain, there are claims that during NDEs, people have been able to hear conversations and see the actions of people around them and even observe things such as the behavior of needles on dials, all of which they could not possibly have known about while in a comatose state. The most famous case of this involves a woman named Maria who apparently saw a shoe on an inaccessible ledge of a hospital in Seattle. The social worker attending her later found this shoe just as Maria had described it.

Stephen Levine, in his widely read book, *Who Dies*, describes the counseling work he does with dying patients. He says that the moment of death is often a moment of great quietude and peace. Somehow there is an okayness that is felt. As one NDEer reported, "death is absolutely safe." What can be sensed is the process of dissolving, which appears to be the predominant physical experience in the transition we call dying. Levine's contribution to his patients was seeped in the spiritual realization that we need to learn to just be present and let go. His efforts and work are impressive; mostly, he escorts dying patients down the path to the transition. We need to take what we've learned from Levine and apply it to those who are younger and healthier, so that their lives could become more meaningful now.

In Tehillim Chapter 23:2,4 David Hamelech said:

"בנאות דשא ירביצני על מי מנוחות ינהלני...גם כי אלך בגיא צלמות לא
אירא רע כי אתה עמדי."

He was at peace of mind in knowing for a fact that God will be at his side while he walks through the valley of the shadow of death and will thus arrive safely on the other side.

In her book entitled *Gifts of a Stranger*, Ahuva Gray tells her own story of how she made her way to convert to Judaism. The Jews embraced the Torah by saying "*Naaseh V'nishma.*" She writes that God offered the Torah to other nations of the world, but they refused it. She mentioned a *midrash* that said that among the gentiles, there were those who, as individuals, were ready to accept the Torah. But they were voted down by the sheer numbers against them. All of those who over the years through today converted to Judaism are exactly those very souls who many years ago did not get the chance to live with the Torah as their life force. God gave those individuals who were ready to accept the Torah thousands of years ago another chance at it by reincarnating them into today's world in order to enjoy and embrace the Torah as Jews. Some say that man can be reincarnated up to three times in order to do the *tikkun* his neshama requires in order to get to the next level of holiness and connectedness to the eternal One. The Zohar (1:186b) states, "As long as a person is unsuccessful in his purpose in this world, the Holy One, blessed be He, uproots him and replants him over and over again."

There is a famous *gemara* (Talmudic passage) in Tractate *Pesachim* 50a in which R' Yosef the son of R' Yehoshua ben Levi fell ill and died, and then (according to Rashi) came back to life shortly thereafter. This is the first case that we know of in all of Jewish literature of someone undergoing a near-death experience. In the US alone, 5% of the population experiences an NDE. In almost all of the documented cases, there are descriptions of wonderfully green pastures with breathtaking views, a bright light, and a meeting with a family member or friends already there, who stand ready to escort new arrivals to their own unique pastoral peaceful place in the eternal world.

In Parashat Ki Tisa Chapter 33 verse 20, Hashem tells Moshe Rabbeinu:

לא תוכל לראות את פני, כי לא יראני האדם וחי.

The Sifri in Parashat B'haalotcha explains this verse as: in this world human beings cannot see the face of God and live – but in the afterlife, human beings will be able to see Me.

Interestingly, in the Haftara of Parashat Naso it says:

"ויהי בעלות הלהב מעל המזבח השמימה ויעל מלאך ה' בלהב המזבח ומנוח ואשתו רואים ויפלו על פניהם ארצה. ולא יסף עוד מלאך ה' להראה אל מנוח ואל אשתו...ויאמר מנוח אל אשתו מות נמות כי אלקים ראינו. ותאמר לו אשתו: לו חפץ ה' להמיתנו לא לקח מידינו עולה ומנחה, ולא הראנו את כל אלה, וכעת לא השמיענו זאת."

Manoach and his wife witnessed an angel of God consumed in fire upon an altar as he was making his way up to the heavens. Manoach turned to his wife and said, 'We are going to die because we saw God.' Whereupon his wife answered, 'If God wanted us to die, He wouldn't have accepted our sacrifice upon the altar in the manner in which He did by allowing us to witness it and still be alive.'

In Bamidbar Rabbah 14 it says that when we were standing as a nation at Mount Sinai to receive the Torah, all those present died in order to be able to hear the first commandment directly from God. One of the proofs brought down for this is from a *gemara* in *Shabbat* 88: R' Yehoshua ben Levi said: after every commandment the souls of the nation departed to the next world. If this is the case, then after the first commandment when everyone died, how did the nation receive the rest of the commandments? The Gemara answers that God covered the nation in a special dew that is destined to be used in the World to Come when all the dead will rise once again. This dew was used then to revive each and every one of those who stood at Mt. Sinai.[3]

In the essay, "Immortality and the Soul," which appears in The *Aryeh Kaplan Reader*, Rabbi Aryeh Kaplan cites philosopher Henri Bergson's suggestion that one of the main functions of the brain is to eliminate activity and awareness rather than produce it. It serves as a type of radar-jamming device for all the sensations and memories that would otherwise overwhelm us if allowed to pour into our minds at once. The brain is thus a kind of reducing valve. With this understanding, imagine the experience of death. Kaplan writes:

> Imagine standing naked before God, with your memory wide open, completely transparent without any jamming mechanism or reducing valve to diminish its force. You will remember everything you did…. The memory of every good deed would be the sublimest of pleasures…. But your memory will also be open to all the things of which you are ashamed. They cannot be rationalized away or dismissed. You will be facing yourself, fully aware of the consequences of all your deeds. We all know the terrible shame and humiliation when one is caught in the act of doing something wrong. Imagine being caught by one's own memory with no place to escape…. (Kaplan 179)

Jewish sources also seem to have anticipated the findings of contemporary science. In *Many Lives, Many Masters*, Catherine, Dr. Brian Weiss's patient, who was treated via hypnotic regressions and revealed remarkable stories of her previous lives, concluded:

---

3.   There are also stories recounted by R' Chaim Vital, the prominent student of R' Luria, also known as the Ari. For one of his more famous stories, see #6 in the next chapter.

"Our task is to learn, to become God-like through knowledge. By knowledge we approach God" (Weiss 218).

At the University of Kentucky, research results from a 15-year study on aging and Alzheimer's disease suggested that a positive emotional state at an early age may ward off disease and may even prolong life. Pathological expression of emotion like depression or hostility can lead to illness. Negative emotional states such as anxiety, hatred, and anger can have a cumulative effect on the body over time. People who turn these negative emotions on and off several times daily are hurting themselves and are more likely to fall victim to heart disease and stroke.

Dr. Irvin Yalom wrote that he conducted research on 80 bereaved spouses and found that one third reported a heightened awareness of their own mortality, and that awareness, in turn, was significantly related to a surge of personal growth. As a result of existential confrontation, they became more mature, aware, and wiser. He heard patients say in group therapy, "What a pity that we had to wait till now, till our bodies were riddled with cancer, to know how to live."

Rav Michel Twerski, in his *hesped* of his son-in-law who died tragically at a young age, asked some very difficult questions: What happened to all our prayers on behalf of the one who was sick? What is the meaning of this rejection by God? What happened to the notion that someone who is on his way to do a mitzvah is protected from harm? What about all of those people who are left behind who depended on him for counseling and guidance? What about all of those great rabbis who assured that everything will be OK? These questions clearly obstruct our ability to find comfort. So how do we conduct ourselves?

We live in an era where we are in control of so much, such as advances in medicine, technology, information systems. At the same time, we cannot dictate how God runs the world. We also are hard pressed to understand the many strange and tragic events that surround us. But we must understand that there is no cause and effect 100% of the time. There is a much deeper calculation at work here. God acts in a loving, purposeful way. If we can accept that through His providence He is caring and shielding us, then we'll know His decision is right. That being the case, what do we do next? What is further demanded of us? The answer, continues Rav Twerski, is that we have to begin to become a student of the deceased. We must figure out how the deceased influenced us as individuals and as a community. We need to be able to let go of the frustration and despair because otherwise it obstructs our ability to absorb what the lessons are that we must learn.

There is a *midrash* in Shir HaShirim that says: כי רבים בני שוממה מבני גאולה – *Times of destruction and loneliness raise more righteousness and saintly people than any other time in our history (even during the time of the Temple).* Are we going to allow ourselves to be destroyed, or will we use this opportunity to create something bigger and better through the deceased being our teacher?

Rabbi Twerski concludes that most of humankind is trapped in mediocrity – they are simply not willing to put forth the effort and the energy to rise up. So they live in a state of stagnation. We look at our dreams and give up because we think it's too hard. If we take a look at sports teams who achieve excellence, we notice that they don't give up on their dream to be champions; they actualize their potential. They won't be denied.

So, too, God looks at us and instilled in each of us the ability to shine – to be a champion at something. We just have to look deeper and realize that we do have this potential and allow it to develop and self-actualize. We need to liberate ourselves from complacency and mediocrity. We need to see adversity as a challenge, as an adventure. If we define it positively, we will appreciate the gifts that we have.

Rav Avigdor Miller quotes Psalms 126:2: אז ימלא שחוק פינו.

What does that mean – *then* we will be filled with joy? It means: Don't laugh too heartily here – because *then* refers to the World to Come. What is he saying here? After all, it is human nature not to look forward to dying. It's our nature to want to live long lives. When Yitzchok Avinu agreed to go to the *mizbeach* (altar), he was happy to do it, but he wasn't exactly looking forward to it. Facing death is one of the most fearsome things that happen to mankind. But it transformed his life. When Yaakov Avinu saw the ladder, it transformed his life. He was one of the most successful people who ever lived and yet despite his good fortune, he mourned many years for Yoseph. It was necessary for him to have this sadness in order for him to live more successfully. God brings death to this world as a sober reminder to us that this world isn't the last stop, so that we shouldn't lose our appetite for the World to Come. Human beings can easily get lost in this world. Even if people have everything, God wants us to still look forward to *olam haba.* Says Rav Miller: Death and grief and suffering are all reminders to us not to get too comfortable here in this world. The pursuit of achievement in this world is correct – it is appropriate to do as many mitzvoth as we can here so that it will serve us in good stead in *olam haba.* But happiness is reserved for the next world. In fact, there is so much happiness around us all the time that it becomes a danger to deceive us into thinking that this world is all there is. We'll say it is a pity we can't go on living forever here, and we forget about the notion of *olam haba.* So God steps in and reminds us of the purpose of our existence.

Sadness causes one to be more successful. Rav Miller continues with the following example: Let's say we have a bout with an illness – can't urinate – we go to the hospital – they put a rubber hose through the small orifice – and it hurts like nothing we've experienced before. Afterwards, when it's taken out and we can urinate normally, we rejoice each time it happens without pain. Rav Miller says: That's true happiness – to function normally. When those suffering from migraines get relief, they are ecstatic. It is an unbelievable feeling.

God gives us a new perspective on ordinary living. God expects us to enjoy the good things life has to offer in this world. But we don't have to go out of our way on a worldly trip to far-out places. All we have to do is appreciate the everyday gifts we were given. When his two sons died, Aaron HaCohen understood that it was a lesson and concentrated on the time when he would see them again.

In conclusion, I'd like to quote a patient of Dr. Michael Sabom's who, after having a heart attack, related his experience during those few moments he was elsewhere: "There is something in the afterlife that is recognizable here in this world. It feels good. I think I was in complete serenity and peace. I didn't want to return here. It was different. There wasn't an absence of life nor an absence of feeling – the feeling was simply outstanding – and full of life. I can't explain it and I cannot explain the form my body took there, but without a doubt, I was very much alive."

As you assimilate what you've read here, I hope you come away with a more positive attitude, filled with a renewed understanding, and armed with the courage and faith to live life here to the fullest, with every expectation that life in the hereafter will be even better.

PART TWO
Bibliotherapy

Overview

Healing Through Reading

*B*ibliotherapy can be defined as the use of books to help people solve problems. Another, more precise definition is that bibliotherapy is a technique for structuring interaction between a facilitator and a participant based on mutual sharing of literature (J.T. Pardeck & J.A. Pardeck).

The idea of healing through books is not a new one – it can be traced far back in history, from the days of the first libraries in Greece (Bibliotherapy Fact Sheet, 1982). Classical scholars, physicians, psychologists, social workers, nurses, parents, teachers, librarians, and counselors, however, have differently interpreted the use of books in healing. There is, in fact, confusion in determining the dividing line between reading guidance and bibliotherapy (Smith). And the vast amount of professional literature that is available on bibliotherapy naturally mirrors the point of view of the helping professional who wrote it and the field in which he or she is an expert.

Riordan and Wilson, in a review of the literature on the effects of bibliotherapy, found that a majority of the studies show mixed results for the efficacy of bibliotherapy as a separate treatment for the solving of problems. They concluded that bibliotherapy generally appears to be more successful as an adjunctive therapy. Despite such mixed research results, however, interest in the use of bibliotherapy appears to have increased in the past few years. This most likely reflects the increase of societal and familial problems in the United States – rise in divorce, alienation of young people, excessive peer group pressure, alcohol and drug abuse, and so on. Educators have also begun to recognize the increasingly critical need for delivering literacy instruction to at-risk and homeless children and their families (Ouzts).

Furthermore, Riordan and Wilson concluded that the explosion of self-help programs during the 1980s has contributed to the rise in the use of bibliotherapy, in the form of popular self-help books, such as *What Color Is Your Parachute* and *The Relaxation Response*. Books such as these are the prescriptive choice of most mental health professionals for their clients, rather than fiction or poetry, according to these two researchers. Nowadays, *The Feeling Good Handbook* by Dr. David Burns is considered to be one of the more popular and successful psychotherapy self-help books. But is self-help (even directed self-help) really bibliotherapy? How do we define the actual technique of bibliotherapy?

Bibliotherapeutic intervention may be undertaken for many reasons: [1] to develop an individual's self-concept; [2] to increase an individual's understanding of human behavior or motivations; [3] to foster an individual's honest self-appraisal; [4] to provide a way for a person to find interests outside of self; [5] to relieve emotional or mental pressure; [6] to show an individual that he or she is not the first or only person to encounter such a problem; [7] to show an individual that there is more than one solution to a problem; [8] to help a person discuss a problem more freely; and [9] to help an individual plan a constructive course of action to solve a problem.

Aristotle believed that literature had *healing* effects and the ancient Romans also recognized that there was some relationship between medicine and reading. Most of the better mental hospitals in Europe had established libraries by the eighteenth century – in the United States by the middle of the nineteenth century. By the early nineteenth century, many physicians had begun to recommend books for the emotional difficulties of the mentally ill. Drs. William and Karl Menninger furthered the use of bibliotherapy by encouraging the growth of the library at the Menninger Clinic. In the field of education, teachers began to utilize bibliotherapy in the 1940s. Today, school media specialists, counselors, librarians, or teachers may incorporate bibliotherapy into their programs. During the 1950s, group reading was added to the treatment of alcoholism. Work in bibliotherapy progressed through the 1960s in such areas as drug addiction, fear, attitudinal changes, moral maturity, death and all exceptionalities (B. Salup & A. Salup).

Dr. Brian Weiss, at the very end of his widely acclaimed book, *Many Lives, Many Masters*, writes: "I hope that you will be helped by what you have read here, that your own fear of death has been diminished, and that the messages offered to you about the true meaning of life will free you to go about living yours to the fullest, seeking harmony and inner peace and reaching out in love to your fellow humans."

Chapter One

Transition

1. God made life such that nothing dies forever. He created nature's life and death cycles and seasons to teach us that physical death and rebirth mirror a spiritual dormancy and rebirth. This keeps us from thinking that death ends our existence. Instead, it marks our transition to a more wonderful life beyond.

(Rabbi Aryeh Kaplan, *Sefer Yetzirah – The Book of Creation*)

2. This world is full of opposites. Without good, there can be no bad. Without bad, there can be no good. In order to appreciate the good, one must experience the bad. Light and darkness – each with its advantages and disadvantages, but at the same time one can appreciate those advantages by recognizing the disadvantages. The same holds true for wisdom and stupidity, rich and poor, laughing and crying, hearing-deafness, cold-hot, purity-defilement, war-peace, man-woman, life and death. If one can appreciate the fact that there is life after life, then life in this world becomes more fun and enjoyable. Death then represents the process by which we walk from one environment into the next.

Moreover, by accepting the fact that we are limited in our bodies in this world, it gives us something to look forward to in the next world where our soul is free to roam around without physical limitations whatsoever.

(Aharon Yellinek, *Sefer Bet Midrash Cheder Rishon*)

3. On the night that a couple have intimate relations, God calls the Angel of Pregnancy and informs him that Mr. A is about to fertilize the egg of Mrs. A. He tells him to go and gather the sperm in a cup and to disperse it on a threshing floor into 365 parts. The angel does this and brings it back to God whereupon the angel asks, "What will become of this drop of sperm?" Immediately God decrees whether it will be strong or weak, long or short, male or female, ignorant or wise, rich or poor, but concerning righteous or wicked God does not decree as it is up to each person to decide. Next God hints to the Angel of the Spirits to bring him a certain holy spirit who resides along with many other holy spirits in their own world. The spirit appears before God and bows down before Him. God tells him to enter into the drop of sperm whereupon the spirit immediately responds by saying: "My God, I am satisfied in the world that I have been in since the day I was created, so please do not make me enter this impure droplet since I am totally pure and holy." God responds by saying to the spirit: The world which you are about to enter is a better place than the one you are coming from. Furthermore, when I created you, I had in mind for you to enter this particular droplet of sperm. Immediately God escorts the spirit into the droplet, whereupon the Angel of Pregnancy comes and implants it in the mother's womb, commissions two other angels to guard it, and they place a candle on the droplet's head. The droplet sees things from the beginning of time until the end of the world. In the morning, the angel escorts him to the Garden of Eden and shows him all of the righteous people (*tzaddikim*) sitting in their full glory, and says to the droplet: "Do you know what sort of spirit was in those *tzaddikim*"? The spirit says "No." The angel then points to one of them and says: "That

particular one had a spirit very similar to yours, and if you lead your life on earth as they did, after moving into the World to Come, you shall join these *tzaddikim* in the glory in which you now see them. However, if you choose not to follow their way, you will end up in a place that I will show you later." That night the angel takes the spirit to visit Hell and shows him wicked people who are constantly being beaten by the Angels of Destruction and proceeds to tell him: This fire will be your fate if you do not follow God's ways. The next day, the angel takes the spirit on a tour of every step he will take during his lifetime on earth, where he will live, where he will be buried, and again shows him the good world and the bad one. That night he returns the spirit to the mother's womb, whereupon he remains for the next nine months. At the end of this period, the same angel appears and says, "Your time has arrived to come out." The spirit still does not want to come out but the angel reminds him that against your will you shall come into this better world. As he is being born, the spirit begins to cry because of the world he is leaving behind. The angel strokes him under the nose and extinguishes the candle above its head, whereupon the spirit promptly forgets all that he was shown.

(Yellinek)

4. Rabbi Berachiah sat and expounded: Each day we speak of the World to Come. Do we then understand what we are saying? In Aramaic, the "World to Come" is translated "the world that came." And what is the meaning of "the world that came"? We learned that before the world was created, it arose in thought to create an intense light to illuminate it. He created an intense light over which no created thing could have authority. The Blessed Holy One saw, however, that the world could not endure [this light]. He therefore took a seventh of it and left it in its place for them. The rest He put away for the righteous in the Ultimate Future. He said, "If they are worthy of this seventh and keep it, I will give them [the rest] in the Final World."

(Rabbi Aryeh Kaplan, *The Bahir,* Part One)

5. One must prepare oneself mentally during one's lifetime; one must create, build up, and cultivate those faculties which one desires to be of deciding influence at death and in the after-death state – in order never to be taken unawares, and to be able to react spontaneously when the critical moment of death has come. This is clearly expressed in the Root Verses as rendered in The Tibetan Book of the Dead:

> "O procrastinating one, who thinketh not of the coming of
>   death,
> Devoting thyself to the useless doings of this life,
> Improvident art thou in dissipating thy great opportunity;
> Mistaken, indeed, will thy purpose be now if thou returnest
>   empty-handed (from this life)…
> *(The Tibetan Book of the Dead)*

6. This selection is from the works of Rabbi Chaim Vital, a student of the Ari HaKadosh. We pick up the storyline two years after the loss of a husband, whose wife is still in a state of depression and bewilderment.

"And in her dream people are running, she being amongst them. They ran beyond the city limits, and entered a dark, thick forest. They continued running when suddenly a bright light came shining through, the forest ended, and the sun was at its peak. Before her in the clearing was a large garden filled with beautiful flowers from which emanated a wonderful scent; encircling the garden was what appeared to be a horizon of teal blue waters. She then noticed a magical-looking, old and bearded Jew clothed in a long white robe. The man asked her if she wanted to see her husband. With a thumping heart, she followed him.

"The man stopped next to a tall tree full of enormous juicy fruit, and in the near distance she saw a golden fenced-in field in which a whole bunch of Jews clad in colorful garb sitting in perfect rows and learning Torah. In their midst stood a young man who was delivering a discourse. 'Wait here a moment,' said the old man, 'as soon as the shiur is over, you will see him.'

"She glanced all around her and couldn't believe her eyes. As soon as the shiur was over, the young man who was teaching began to walk towards her. She immediately recognized the overcoat as being that of her husband's, she became dizzy with the thought that her (late) husband was indeed standing there before her.

"When she regained her composure, she opened her eyes and asked him: 'Why did you leave me at such a young age?'

"'You should know,' he began in a pleasant voice, 'that the world you live in is a land of decrees where people are sent in order to complete certain tasks left unfinished, or to suffer from sins committed in an earlier lifetime. The real world is right here. Know, that I was already in your world before I met you, I was a great scholar and tzaddik, but I didn't want to get married and have children so as not to be distracted from my learning. When I left your world, I was offered to be the Rosh Yeshiva (Headmaster) in The Garden of Eden, and I thus began to go higher and higher spiritually. When it was known to others here that I had not married nor had children, I was sent back to your world in order to do these things, and that's how I met you. When our seventh child was born, I was called up to the next world again in order to resume my duties in the yeshiva, where all of my students were awaiting my return. Great was your merit for being my wife for I have a good name here, and when the right time comes, we will again live harmoniously together, here in this world.'

"'But,' she said, 'I didn't know that you were such a scholar; you never really had much time to learn when we were married.' Her husband replied: 'I also didn't know, since my purpose for coming down to your world was to complete a part of my soul that had been missing, that is to get married, have children and to support them properly. When I came back to the next world, my head was immediately filled again with unlimited Torah knowledge.'"

(Rabbi Chaim Vital, *Writings of Rav Chaim Vital*)

7. There is a certain point at which we must take pause and realize that there are powers and other celestial elements at work here that are beyond our mortal comprehension. The moment we accept the fact that we are limited in this world and cannot see the picture from a global perspective, then we are more likely to cease asking the kinds of questions that in the end, no answer would be satisfactory enough.

This being the case, then how do we continue and deal with the deep void left behind, the piercing hurt that lingers after the death of a son? Where do we find solace if we can't reach understanding of the Creator's master plan?

We live in a world that is described as a corridor, a preparatory room, a place where we are sort of practicing before meriting the next world. In other words, there is life after life. What is death? It is a mere technical process that allows us mortals to gain entry to the next world. Just as a fetus in its mother's womb is in another world, the birth process itself allows one to reach the world we know here. Likewise, Gadi moved along from this world to a different world where he is benefiting from the pleasure of divine light. This means, clearly, that he continues to live! In Judaism, there is no such concept as dying followed by darkness, and that's the end of the ballgame. We believe that there exists a whole world out there in all its glory and peacefulness, in which one can enjoy a high level of spiritual living – one that is impossible to know in this world. But it emphatically does exist – it is vital to believe that Gadi is now in such a place.

(Spoken at Memorial Service for 19-year-old Gedalia Natan Kastner, of blessed memory, Jerusalem, May 2004)

8. Upon returning home, we all went in for an afternoon nap. I actually managed to fall asleep – and I started to dream. I was able to recall the dream in full detail.

I was standing atop a mountain – although it felt like I was in a hotel – I wasn't alone – there were many people about – I looked down toward the courtyard of the hotel and I saw a bunch of men and women lined up for a relay race. There were at least ten people standing at the start line awaiting the sound of the gun. The path was a straight one but it was known to all present that there were mines along the path. Once a runner steps on a mine, he is automatically disqualified. These mines were not of the real kind that can blow you to pieces. It was an artificial one designed for the sake of the race. One of the runners was Gadi. He was standing in lane number 1, the farthest away from my vantage point above. But I had no doubt it was him. The judge gave the signal, and the runners were off, albeit very slowly and deliberately so as not to come in contact with a mine. Suddenly, after about a minute, Gadi burst forward as if there were no mines to worry about ahead. When he got to about the halfway point, the other runners, seeing that Gadi started sprinting, also began to kick into high gear. Toward the finish line, a number of challengers came close to Gadi but were unable to overtake him, except for a woman in the next lane who thought that she had won the race. From where I was standing, it looked to me like Gadi won the race, but the woman began jumping up and down, her hands held high above her head, and began her victory trot. The other runners began forming a circle around her in line to congratulate her feat. Gadi stood in the distance hardly believing what was taking place. The woman then ran over to the judge to claim her prize, but the judge shook his head "no," and began to make his way toward Gadi. With a broad smile and a heart filled with joy, the judge proclaimed Gadi the winner and proceeded to give him no less than three prizes.

When I saw this, my heart swelled with happiness, but I noticed that Gadi was having a hard time negotiating the three prizes as he was walking back to his hotel room. He was walking with the familiar awkward gait that he had in this world. I immediately felt the need to help him, so I ran to the elevator and went down to the main floor. Upon getting out of the elevator, I started hurrying toward the courtyard, but because there were so many people milling around, I lost my way. Fortunately, there was a mini-bus that offered to take me to him, so I got on. The driver was a well-known rabbi of a *shul*. I thought that within a moment we would get to the spot where Gadi was, but the driver also lost his way and we found ourselves in the middle of nowhere, our cellphones out of range from making any further contact with the hotel. I then awoke.

It is still unclear what all the elements of dream mean. What I can say for sure, is that Gadi indeed won. Despite the fact that we didn't speak in the dream, and I had a hard time trying to get to him after the race, he gave me a message. He showed me that he is doing well despite what seemed to be obstacles in his way. A whole year passed by and I hadn't had a dream like this, although during the *shloshim* (Judaism's thirty-day mourning period following the death of a family member) I did have a dream with Gadi in it but the story and circumstances were entirely different. A whole year we didn't receive any messages – and now, smack in the middle of *Shavuot* (The Feast of Weeks), the day that Gadi began his journey to the next world, he returned to me in a dream that was as clear as a bell. The feeling I got upon awakening was one of total comfort.

We never cease "being." The destiny of each neshama in the world is to do its tikkun in the physical world and then return to the bright light in the sky and continue to live its life in the eternal spiritual world. And maybe, in saying good-bye to a loved one, one would see that certain kinds of loss are inevitable and natural and don't need to be feared. Maybe I could see that loss is a part of life, which includes birth, growth and change, finally death, and that all those things are good, the whole thing is good, even the pain and fear that are a part of it.

(author's communication, May 26, 2004)

9. There was a head of a family living in a place in the country of the Northumbrians known as Cunningham, who led a devout life with his entire household. He fell ill and grew steadily worse until the crisis came, and in the early hours of one night he died. But at

daybreak he returned to life and suddenly sat up to the great con-
sternation of those weeping around the body, who ran away; only
his wife, who loved him more dearly, remained with him, though
trembling and fearful. The man reassured her and said: "Do not
be frightened; for I have truly risen from the grasp of death, and
I am allowed to live among men again. But henceforward I must
not live as I used to, and must adopt a very different way of life."
Not long afterward, he abandoned all worldly responsibilities and
entered the monastery of Melrose, which is almost completely
surrounded by a bend in the river Tweed.

This was the account he used to give of his experience:

A handsome man in a shining robe was my guide, and we
walked in silence in what appeared to be a northeasterly
direction. As we traveled onward, we came to a very broad
and deep valley of infinite length.... He soon brought me
out of darkness into an atmosphere of clear light, and as he
led me forward in bright light, I saw before us a tremendous
wall which seemed to be of infinite length and height in all
directions. As I could see no gate, window, or entrance in
it, I began to wonder why we went up to the wall. But when
we reached it, all at once – I know not by what means – we
were on top of it. Within lay a very broad and pleasant
meadow.... Such was the light flooding all this place that it
seemed greater than the brightness of daylight or of the sun's
rays at noon....

[The guide said,] 'You must now return to your body
and live among men once more; but, if you will weigh your
actions with greater care and study to keep your words and
ways virtuous and simple, then when you die you too will win
a home among these happy spirits that you see. For, when I
left you for a while, I did so in order to discover what your
future would be.' When he told me this, I was most reluctant
to return to my body; for I was entranced by the pleasant-
ness and beauty of the place I could see and the company

I saw there. But I did not dare to question my guide, and meanwhile, I know not how, I suddenly found myself alive among men once more.

This man of God would not discuss these and other things that he had seen with any apathetic or careless-living people, but only with those who were haunted by fear of punishment or gladdened by the hope of eternal joys, and were willing to take his words to heart and grow in holiness.

(The Venerable Bede, 673–735 C.E., an English monk, *A History of the English Church and People*)

10. We go through many stages when we're here. We shed a baby body, go into a child's, from a child to an adult, an adult into old age. Why shouldn't we go one step beyond and shed the adult body and go on to a spiritual plane?

(Dr. Brian Weiss, *Many Lives, Many Masters*)

11. Think of the transition between the terrible grief of going from Israel's Memorial Day directly into the incredible joy of Independence Day as if you are moving from the dimension of death to the dimension beyond death.

(author unknown)

12. The Kabbalah is filled with mentions of the spiritual body, which is likened to a "garment of the soul" (*Sefer Hagilgulim*). Those who are about to come down into this world are dressed with garments – with faces and bodies – like those in this world…. When they actually enter this world they take off their spiritual garments and put on the garments of this world…. When it is time for them to leave this world, the garment of the body is taken off, and they put back on the garment that they had to divest themselves of when they entered this world.

(*Zohar* II: 150a)

13. When the soul separates itself from its physical body at death, it has the ability and desire to go back and forth between two places; the physical world and the spiritual world. For the first three days after death, the soul believes that it can somehow re-enter its body.[4] During the shiva period (7 days of mourning in Jewish practice) the soul goes forth and returns from its home on earth to its paradise-like home and from its paradise-like home to its former home.

(*Pirkei D'Rabbi Eliezer*)

14. The entranceway into paradise is the cave described in Genesis where Abraham buried Sarah, which is situated in Hebron. When Abraham entered to inspect the cave before he bought it, he saw a door open to paradise and a shining light that literally lit up the cave. People travel through this cave when they pass out of this world.

(*Zohar* 1:127a)

15. I saw myself lifted out of physical body…it was as if a whole lot of loving beings were taking all the tired parts out of me, similar to car mechanics in a car repair shop. It was as if they were replacing every tired and worn-out part of my physical body with a new, fresh, energized part. I experienced a great sense of peace and serenity, a feeling of literally being taken care of, of having no worry in the world. I also had an incredible sense that once all the parts were replaced, I would be as young and fresh and energetic as I had been prior to this…

(Dr. Elisabeth Kubler Ross, *On Death and Dying*)

16. One also sees relatives and friends already there. They appear and look the same as they did in this world, and he recognizes

---

4.   According to Astor, this may be an indication of the deep psychological need to deny death.

them all. They then escort him to his unique dwelling place in heaven.

(*Zohar*, Vayehi 218:2)

17. Our Sages view death not as an end, but as a new birth. A farmer plants a seed in the ground. There, the shell around the kernel decays. The body around the seed decomposes, allowing a new plant to come forth. The essence of the seed, the kernel, is preserved, but it too must disappear in its present form before it can give birth to the ultimate goal – a shoot growing into a plant. The spiritual concept hinted at by this process is that sometimes the outer shell must "die" so that the inner essence can be expressed.

Spring, too, serves as a metaphor for the new birth we call the afterlife. For months it is dark and gloomy; everything is frozen or sleeping. Shortly thereafter the world begins to fill with blossoming flowers and chirping birds. What had seemed like death turns out to have been a period of transition during which the world was preparing for a spurt of new life.

(Rabbi Yitzchok Kirzner, *Making Sense of Suffering*)

18. Suppose there were twin brothers lying together in the womb who could think and ask each other what would happen to them once they left their mother's womb. They would not be able to form any conception whatsoever of what awaited them. Let us imagine that one of them believed in the tradition which he had received, that there was a future life beyond the womb, while the other, a "rational being," would only accept what his own intelligence could grasp and he, accordingly, of "this world" alone. The two would disagree and argue, very much as men do on Earth – some believing that man continues to live; others denying that man has any life other than in this world of the present. Suppose that the "believing" brother were to repeat what had been transmitted to him, that with their emergence from the womb they would enter a new and more spacious realm, that they would eat through their mouths, see distant objects with their eyes, and hear

with their ears, that their legs would straighten, that they would stand erect and traverse vast distances on a gigantic nurturing earth, replete with oceans, rivers, etc., who only believed in what he could sense, would jeer at his brother's naivete, in indulging in such fantasies. He would retort that only a fool would believe all of this nonsense, which makes no sense to the rational mind. The more the "believer" would elaborate on the variegated features they would encounter in this world, the more would the "rational" brother mock and ridicule him. The believing brother would ask, "What, then, my enlightened brother, do you believe is in store for us when we leave the womb?"

"Simple and obvious. Once this enclosure opens and you are torn away from this world where your food and drink are provided, you will fall into an abyss from which there is no return. You might as well never have existed at all," the 'rational' brother would reply.

In the heat of their argument, the womb suddenly opens. The "naïve" brother slips and falls outside. Remaining within, the other brother is shattered by the "tragedy" that has overtaken his brother. "Brother, where are you? How did you manage to fall to your destruction? Your folly that these contractions were birth-pangs caused your downfall. That is why you did not clutch at anything to stop yourself." As he moans the misfortune, his ears catch the cry of his brother, and he trembles. To him this spells the end, the last gasp of his expiring brother…Outside, at that very moment, joy and celebration fill the home of the newly born baby: "Mazel tov, mazel tov, a baby…we have a son!"

(Rabbi Yechiel Tucazinsky, Gesher Hachaim – The Bridge of Life)

19. Some descriptions of the transcendental environment as expressed by patients of Dr. Sabom:

* beautiful flowers in a flowerbed
* steps leading to the golden gates of heaven

* a beautiful park with hill, trees and flowers
* just another world, bright, sunny, real beautiful
* a still stream of water with rainbow colors in background
* a beautiful blue sky...a field of flowers of different colors
* everything was silver like diamonds and stars
* walking on clouds during a clear, beautiful summer day
* water with a beautiful sunglow...trees...shadows of gold
* a place of beautiful light that pulsated with exquisite music
* a long corridor which became all light
* gates of heaven with people on the other side of the gate
* a fence dividing extremely scraggly territory from the most beautiful pastoral scene
* a landscape full of people of all different nationalities all working on their arts and crafts
* the top of a mountain...just beautiful up there...ethereal beauty
* flowers, trees of all kinds, beautiful flower gardens, the sun was beautiful...a tremendous happiness thing
* a beautiful panorama...just beyond words
* a beautiful green pasture...cattle grazing...bright sunshiny day

(Dr. Michael Sabom, *Recollections of Death*)

20. I have a friend...who often volunteers as a clown for dying children in the hospitals in San Francisco...He told me that when he is with a dying child he says something like, "You know, look at this body. You can see that it's really not much use. It's not strong enough to ride a bicycle. It can't play ball. It can't go out and skip rope. In fact, you can't even go to school. When your body falls away, you'll be just fine. And you'll probably see a light. If the light goes left, go left. If the light goes right, go right. That's all there is to it."

(Stephen Levine, *Who Dies*)

21. Perhaps the first recognition in the process of acknowledging, opening, and letting go that we call "conscious dying" is when we begin to see that we are not the body...We see that we have a body but it is not who we are. Just as one may have an overcoat but that is not you...when it is spring one doesn't need the overcoat any more. One puts it aside or sends it to the dry cleaner.

(Levine)

22. A doctor friend was telling me that he had pronounced nineteen people dead that month and that it was getting to be a bit much for him. He said he was conditioned to help patients, to "do something," but that there was nothing he could do under these circumstances, that they were "already dead." "Only their body is dead," I said. "There is still something that might be useful to them." So now to every patient he works with who dies, he says silently, from his heart, "Let go. Go on. You have only died. Don't be confused. Let love guide you. Let go into the light." He says he doesn't know if it does them any good, but it does something very useful for him.

(Levine)

23. If someone goes into a coma, stay with that person and talk with him. He is present. Indeed, coma is like being on the mezzanine level. You are not yet on the second floor, but you have a whole different perspective of the first floor. Talking with that person either aloud or silently through the heart seems to give a relative point by which they can see that they are not who they imagined themselves to be, that consciousness is not limited to the body.

(Levine)

24. The body is like a light bulb, which is lit one minute and dark the next because the current running through it is withdrawn and leaves it gray and empty. The light bulb is the same – only the

45

current which made it functional has departed. The body dies but the spirit that transcends it cannot be touched by death.

(Levine)

25. In many afterdeath systems the first place described – the first stop after death takes place – is a Waiting Place. Since a profound crossing into a new reality has just taken place, it requires that there be a stopping, a waiting, a resting place. There is familiarity with this new reality as revered ancestors and friends are encountered. The utter familiarity of place and inhabitants counters the fear of the unknown, and the petrifying vision of nothingness is avoided. The purpose of this Waiting Place is to provide a place where rest is possible, fear abates, and the traveler prepares for the trip onward.

(Dr. Sukie Miller, *After Death*)

Chapter Two

Near Death Experience

1. No matter what we do, though, the question will not go away. Life will always remind us – sometimes gently, sometimes more forcibly – about the possibility of death. Perhaps our greatest fear about dying is thinking that it is a total separation from our loved ones and the end of our existence. People who know that there is an afterlife where they will meet their loved ones and God are not afraid of death. Physicians such as Elisabeth Kubler-Ross, Melvin Morse, and Raymond Moody have documented many stories of people who have had near-death experiences (NDES). NDEers' souls have journeyed into the afterlife, then returned to life here. Not only aren't they afraid to die, they affirm for us that there is a spiritual world beyond.

Many had been clinically dead for as long as two minutes, five minutes, even ten minutes and more. These people did not experience a black nothingness, but rather a very rich, vivid set of sensations. They typically go through at least some of the following: They feel their souls separate from and hover over their bodies as they watch everything happening to and around them. They initially feel disoriented as they view their lifeless body and the people who are trying to rescue them. They may also see people who are farther away, such as relatives in a waiting room or a nurse getting medication down the hallway, as well as machinery that is being used to revive them that is out of their field of vision. When people try to resuscitate them, their souls don't want to return to their bodies. They are happy and peaceful outside their bodies and have no desire to return to the physical world. Their souls feel utter joy, bliss, and serenity as they travel through a dark tunnel or climb a staircase toward a brilliant light. They enter a world of beauty where the souls of deceased friends, relatives, or religious figures greet them. They feel indescribable pleasure and happiness in this spiritual world where everything is bathed in love and total understanding. Once they meet it, their souls want to be with it forever. Time and space cease to exist, and they know that they are confronting eternity. The Being takes many adults through a life review, showing them everything that they did. Meanwhile, they feel the effects of each of their actions on others. They realize that love and knowledge are two of the most important things that there are. At some point, the Being or the souls that greet the new arrival explain that it is not yet time for it to stay there. Nevertheless, it is either given a choice to stay forever, or told that it must return to its body. Even though NDEers don't want to return, they go back to their bodies anyway.

From a strict medical viewpoint, they should have seen or felt nothing. Yet, not only could they see and feel, but they experienced sensations that were larger than life, as described above including floating above their bodies and watching brave efforts on the part of others to revive them, traveling through a type of tunnel, and encountering deceased relatives or beings of light, or experiencing an all-encompassing warm, restorative light. People who have had these experiences no longer fear death. They know that they have an eternal soul and a task to fulfill on earth before returning to a world of indescribable goodness.

(Dr. Raymond Moody, *Reflections on Life After Life*; Rabbi Aryeh Kaplan, *Immortality and the Soul*)

2. About 95% of the NDEers indicate they do not fear death, or have a greatly reduced fear of death.

(Jeffrey Long, M.D., *After Death Communication Research Foundation*)

3. After crossing over to the "other side," you will see the essence of a being in the form of a bright light which exudes a tremendous amount of loving energy. You will communicate via an exchange of thoughts. You will then see your entire past flash in front of you with much speed and in great, wondrous detail. Your friends and relatives who have already crossed over shall come and greet you. (These statements, reported by those who had near death experiences, are also found in various places in the Torah). We are given permission to see things that in our current lives we do not have permission to see.

(Rabbi Avigdor Miller, *Tiferet Gadi Tape Library*)

4. The Talmud cites two cases in which a person returned from clinical death. In *Bava Batra* 10b, Rav Yosef, the son of Rav Yehoshua, passed away and came back to life. His father asked him: What did you see? He responded: An upside-down world. Those who were considered in this world to be respected and rich were lowly there, and those who are lowly here were on the highest spiritual level there. Whereupon his father said: You saw clearly indeed. In *Rosh Hashana* 17a, Rav Huna, son of Rav Yehoshua, came back to life and told Rav Papa who said to him: Because you always treated others by giving them the benefit of the doubt, here too you were not judged according to the exact letter of the law, and hence you were given latitude in meriting more years of life in this world.

5. A man is dying and, as he reaches the point of greatest physical distress, he hears himself pronounced dead by his doctor. He begins to hear an uncomfortable noise, a loud ringing or buzzing, and at the same time feels himself moving very rapidly through a long tunnel. After this, he suddenly finds himself outside of his own physical body, but still in the immediate physical environment, and he sees his own body from a distance, as though he is a spectator. He watches the resuscitation attempt from this unusual vantage point and is in a state of emotional upheaval. After a while, he collects himself and becomes more accustomed to his odd condition. He notices that he still has a "body," but one of a very different nature and with very different powers from the physical body he has left behind. Soon other things begin to happen. Others come to meet and to help him. He glimpses the spirits of relatives and friends who have already died, and a loving, warm spirit of a kind he has never encountered before – a being of light – appears before him. This being asks him a question, non-verbally, to make him evaluate his life and helps him along by showing him a panoramic, instantaneous playback of the major events of his life. At some point he finds himself approaching some sort of barrier or border, apparently representing the limit between earthly life and the next life. Yet, he finds that he must go back to earth, that the time for his death has not yet come. At this point he resists, for by now he is taken up with his experiences in the afterlife and does not want to return. He is overwhelmed by intense feelings of joy, love, and peace. Despite his attitude, though, he somehow reunites with his physical body and lives. Later he tries to tell others, but he has trouble doing so. In the first place, he can find no human words adequate to describe these unearthly episodes. He also finds that others scoff, so he stops telling other people. Still, the experience affects his life profoundly, especially his views about death and its relationship to life.

(Raymond Moody, M.D., *Life After Life*)

6. Dr. Raymond Moody said that everyone he interviewed came

from within the Judeo-Christian tradition. With regard to those who had a near-death experience, he said that it would be almost impossible to determine the degree of prior religious belief in these cases, since everyone in our society is at least exposed to religious concepts. In view of this, the question would always arise for any person to what degree – even unconsciously – he already holds to religious concepts. The persons interviewed who stated that they had no particular religious beliefs prior to their near-death experiences, did state that after having this experience they now accept as true the religious doctrines of a hereafter.

7. Research has shown that survivors of a near-death experience are almost all changed for the good. They grow up to be physically healthier and have fewer psychosomatic complaints. They are happier, exhibit stronger family ties, show more zest for living, and have a greatly diminished fear of death. Similarly, they tend to do more community work, give more charity, and often work in professions that involve helping people. Even those who had a near-death experience as the result of a suicide attempt were found to be significantly less likely to try it again.

(Dr. Melvin Morse and Paul Perry,
Transformed by the Light)

8. King David talks of his total faith in the Shepherd Who he knows is with him though he cannot see Him, and though he is alone in complete darkness. Similarly those who had a near-death experience report that the tunnel they see is a separation between themselves and God (or heaven or their perception of paradise). Death is all around and yet they are strangely comforted – they are confident that there is a light at the end of the tunnel. Instead of a light, some have given accounts of lush fields and other beautiful pastoral scenes. King David relates to this very point by saying how the Shepherd "lays me down in green pastures and leads me beside tranquil waters" (Psalm 23). That knowledge gives him the fortitude to walk through the valley of the shadow of death

with confidence and tranquility. It is the comforting paradise that awaits him upon passage through that valley.

(Yaakov Astor, *Soul Searching*)

9. I don't go to funerals. I don't send flowers. I don't tell people I'm sorry. Somebody tells me somebody died and I say we should be happy. Why don't we have parties at death?...There is something after life. It is a good feeling. [During the NDE] I think I was at total peace with myself. I didn't want to come back. It was different. It was not void of life or feeling, because it was a beautiful feeling, and it was a life. Whatever life it was, whatever form we were in, we existed.

(Patient who underwent an NDE in Dr. Michael Sabom's *Recollections of Death*)

10. The following are typical responses by NDEers who felt they had a "message" for others:

*If people would accept death and that it's not a frightening experience, that it's going to happen and they're going to have to experience it one day, then they would live their life a lot easier.

*I'd be quick to say to you that I don't worry about it [death] because when the time comes there will be a total sense of peace pervade all of your thinking and it will be a very restful feeling.

*That's the advice I give to anyone dying, not to cry or scream...I don't cry when anyone passes away. I know that their pain is gone.

(Sabom)

Chapter Three

World of Souls

1. Our soul lives forever. Our bodies are temporary, yet they provide our souls a house from which it seeks perfection. Actually, the connection between our soul and our body is not temporary at all, since at the time of the Resurrection of the Dead the soul re-enters our body and hence becomes one complete being.
   (Aharon Yellinek, *Sefer Bet Midrash Cheder Rishon*)

2. Sometimes the soul enters into another body before the Resurrection, in order to complete a task or tasks in this world. According to the Zohar and kabbalists, many souls return after it has been in a body that has passed on, and reincarnates into another body in order to fix a flaw from a previous lifetime. Hence, a soul can have more than one reincarnation.
   (Yellinek)

3. Be fervent in my funeral eulogy for I will be standing there (Rav to Rabbi Eliezer, Shabbat 153). The soul knows everything said

about him. That is why delivering a proper, respectful eulogy is highly important. The soul also derives much pleasure from light. On the *yahrzeit*, the soul has permission to travel about the world. When it comes to his former home and sees the light burning, it gets spiritual satisfaction from it.

(Rabbi Chaim Goldberg, *Mourning in Halacha*)

4. This life is a time of development for the soul. The Midrash (*Devarim Rabba* 11:6) in describing the last moments of Moses' life (he was 120 years old), tells us that he begged and pleaded with God to let him live longer. Was Moses afraid to die? After all, how could this be since not only did he know he was eternal but knew that after his death, he would have the opportunity to get even closer to God?

Imagine you were told that you would be allowed into a diamond mine for one hour to pick up all the diamonds you could find. It's hot and stuffy. You are grimy and covered with dirt. Your feet ache, and your back feels like it's breaking, but when that hour is up you beg to have a few extra minutes, because the temporary discomfort is worth the unique opportunity to collect as many diamonds as you can.

(Yaakov Astor, *Soul Searching*)

5. Right before the moment of passing to the next world, as the soul gets ready to leave the body, the soul is given permission to see an overall perspective from above, just as it was given a tour of a similar perspective before entering the body before birth, and in that moment the ultimate spirit engulfs him and shows him what is to transpire in the future (his reward in the World to Come). Then God reveals himself to the soul, and out of sheer ecstasy and desire to connect with its holiness, the soul begins drawing nearer by leaving the body. This is why many times we see the eyes of the deceased remain open during the passing process because of the wonderful, glorious image he just saw. He also is in a state of calmness, satisfaction, and comfort knowing that he is being

taken care of very well. Hence it is incumbent upon those who are present to close the deceased's eyes so as not to "see" something that is less noble than what he just saw.

(Zohar, Vayehi, 226:1, also *Midrash Rabba – Chaye Sarah* 62:2)

6. Dying is not a sudden occurrence – it is a process. When someone dies in a car crash, it seems immediate and sudden. However, even in such a case, the separation of the soul from the body is a slow continuous process that begins 30 days before the actual day of passing. Before the soul leaves, it visits with each and every body part and "says" its good-byes one by one. And only after completing the process of saying goodbye will the soul then leave the body.

(Zohar, Naso 126:2)

7. The purpose of life must be evaluated in terms of our soul. The measure of events in this world is the opportunity they provide to bring out the capacities of the soul. The capacity of the soul determines how much of God's goodness it will absorb in the World to Come.

(Rabbi Yitzchok Kirzner, *Making Sense of Suffering*)

8. If the soul is the essence of our humanity, why did God make it so difficult to attain an awareness of that soul and so easy to focus on our immediate, sensory existence?

We are given a soul in an underdeveloped state, and it is our task to develop that soul through its contact with the world. We create a relationship with our soul, and in doing so we create ourselves as expressions of it. Only by struggling to define ourselves in terms of the soul do we gain possession of our souls. Only by overcoming barriers placed in our path does the soul become something earned and thus our own.

(Kirzner)

9. Even though we will die, our souls whisper to us that a spiritual

part of us will live forever. This keeps us from becoming immobilized by a sense of futility about life.

(Pirkei D'Rabbi Eliezer)

10. A MISSION FULFILLED (to those who suffered a miscarriage):
I would like to express a number of thoughts which I hope will, to a certain degree, ease your situation. It is possible that my words will offer you nothing new, but my feelings of sympathy impel me to try.

Each morning we recite the "Elokai Neshamah" blessing, in which we refer to HaShem as "Lord of all Works, *Master* of all Souls." Later, at the conclusion of the Pesukei D'Zimrah portion of Shacharis, we speak of HaShem as the "*Creator* of all Souls." Why is it that in reference to the neshama, HaShem is referred to first as "*Master*" and then as a "*Creator*"?

To answer this question, we must first understand the following teachings of our Sages which are explained in the writings of the great tzaddikim of later generations. In Heaven, there is a *Heichal HaNeshamos*, Sanctuary of Souls, the source which all neshamos come. Our Sages state that the Final Redemption will not come until all the souls have left this heichal and descended to this world (Yevamos 62a). Each neshama has its own unique mission to fulfill on this world, and is allotted the life-span necessary to fulfill that mission.

Some neshamos belong to a very exalted class. They are of such sublime nature, so holy, sparkling and brilliant, that they simply cannot bear to exist in this world even for a short time. However, they too must leave the *Heichal HaNeshamos* so that it will be emptied, and for other reasons known only to HaShem.

And so HaShem chooses a particular couple who will draw such a neshama down to this world. It departs its place near the Throne of Glory and is immediately placed in an environment in which it is at home – an environment which is heavenly in nature. A woman who is with child carries within herself not only a child, but an entire Gan Eden as well. A flame from the hidden light of Creation shines above the child's head, and by that light the child sees from one end of the world to the other. A heavenly angel learns the entire Torah with the child. All this occurs with every Jewish child.

However, those special neshamos of which we have spoken cannot bear to separate themselves from their sublime existence and sully themselves by living on this earthly world. And so they are spared this discomfort and are returned to their Father in Heaven, having fulfilled their mission by leaving the *Heichal HaNeshamos*, and residing within their mother, thus bringing the world one step closer to the Final Redemption.

And what of the mother, who had endured, hoped and in the end was so terribly disappointed?

She is of flesh and blood and her feelings are understandable. However, in loftier moments, in moments when her intellect can overcome her emotions, the mother can free herself of her earthly thoughts and can share in the elation enjoyed by her neshama. Then she will become infused by a feeling of true joy – the joy of a wealthy person who takes reckoning of all his business endeavors and sees that his profits far outweigh his losses.

She has merited to have had as her guest a pure, holy neshama, accompanied by a heavenly light, a heavenly angel and a heavenly Torah. The Ribono Shel Olam had created a *beis midrash* (house of study) for this neshama within her. And when this neshama left her, some of the *kedushah* (holiness) that had entered her remained, and will not leave her for the rest of her life.

She has merited bringing Mashiach's arrival closer by offering a sacrifice for this purpose. She is not left with a mother's usual compensation; all that she has endured has been for the sake of HaShem and His people, not for her personal joy and satisfaction. She has served not as a worker who awaits immediate payment, but as a loyal soldier, who is ready to suffer wounds in battle, if necessary, solely for the glory of the King.

Was it all worth it?

In painful moments when disappointment sets in and normal human feelings dominate one's mood, the answer may be negative. However, when holiness breaks through, when the intellect of the neshama speaks and the joy of the Jewish soul burst forth, then there is an answer of an entirely different nature. This answer is accompanied by the song of triumph, the joy of the victor, the deep-rooted satisfaction of one who has earned something of immeasurable value.

In the *Heichal HaNeshamos*, the Jewish souls are figuratively speaking, children of HaShem. That sanctuary is their source, and their Father in Heaven is their Creator. When they descend to this world clothed in human form they are seen as servants, with HaShem as their Master.

In the morning, when we arise from our slumber and are still mired in our earthliness, when the physical part of our beings prevails we say, I gratefully thank you...Lord of all works, Master of all neshamos. In effect we are saying, "You, Ribono Shel Olam, Who directs this world with exacting Providence, a world in which every occurrence is a part of Your eternal plan, You are the One Who determines the destiny of every neshama, in harmony with Your Master Plan."

However, following the recitation of Pesukei D'Zimrah and the Song of the Sea, we raise ourselves above the "there exists no 'I.'" Then the Ribono Shel Olam is not seen as the Master over His servants, but rather as the Creator of us, His children. Then we can also perceive HaShem as Creator of certain special neshamos – those that fulfill their mission without having to be seen as servants, clothed in earthly bodies.

In the early morning, our frame of mind permits us only to recite a berachah for a neshamah that resides within a body. It is only later, in the midst of the *Shacharis* (morning) prayers, when we are in an uplifted state, that we can express a blessing even for those sparkling neshamos that are too sublime to enter into this earthly world.

One should realize that the term "miscarriage" is not found in a believing Jew's dictionary. The term implies that one's efforts have ended in failure, that all has been in vain. This is incorrect, for when a Jewish woman conceives it is never in vain. (Moreover, a child will merit *techias hameisim* (resurrection of the dead) even if its life was terminated immediately following conception – See Igros Moshe, Yoreh Deah iii s.138)

May the Ribono Shel Olam grant you nachas and good health. May you merit bringing into this world and raise healthy children and grandchildren who will toil in Torah study and mitzvos. May you and your husband derive much joy and satisfaction from your family and together escort your children to the wedding chupah with joy and feelings of gratitude to the One Above. May you, along with all of Klal Yisrael, merit greeting Mashiach – whose arrival you have brought closer.

(Rabbi Moshe Wolfson, Mashgiach Ruchani of Mesivta
Torah Vadaath and Rav of Congregation Emunas Yisrael,
Brooklyn, in *Vistas of Challenge*, Seryl Sander, ed., ArtScroll)

11. When the son of Rabbi Yochanan ben Zakai died, Rabbi Yochanan's disciples came to (try to) console him. His disciple Rabbi Eliezer entered and said, "The first man (Adam) had a son who died, and he was consoled. You also should accept consolation."

"Not only do I have my personal suffering, but now you remind me of the first man's suffering," said Rabbi Yochanan.

His disciple Rabbi Yehoshua entered and said, "Eyov (Job) had sons and daughters and they all died, and he was consoled."

"Not only do I have my personal suffering, but now you remind me of Eyov's suffering," said Rabbi Yochanan.

His disciple Rabbi Yosi entered and said, "Aharon had two great sons and they both died on the same day, and he was consoled. You also should accept consolation."

"Not only do I have my personal suffering, but now you remind me of Aharon's suffering," said Rabbi Yochanan.

His disciple Rabbi Shimon entered and said, "David, the King, had a son who died and he was consoled, you also should accept consolation."

"Not only do I have my personal suffering, but now you remind me of David's suffering," said Rabbi Yochanan.

Rabbi Elazar ben Arach entered and said, "I will give an analogy to your situation. The king entrusted a precious object with one of his subjects. The subject was in a state of constant worry: 'When will I be able to return the object undamaged and unsoiled to the king?' My teacher, you are in a similar situation. You had a son who was a Torah scholar and left this world without sin. Be consoled that you have returned him in the perfect state that which the King entrusted you."

"Elazar, my son, you have properly comforted me," said Rabbi Yochanan.

(Avot D'Rebbe Natan 14)

Chapter Four

Reincarnation

1. It is not necessarily so that a complete soul reincarnates. A spark of that soul can separate itself from the essence of the soul and enter into a body.

        (Aharon Yellinek, *Sefer Bet Midrash Cheder Rishon*)

2. There is a story told of a young girl who was traveling with her parents to a far and unknown land, a place where none of them had visited before. When they arrived in the city, the young girl suddenly remembered that once upon a time she rode on a horse and buggy that used to take her to a particular house. They found such a carriage in town, boarded it, and proceeded to a house in the country. When she recognized the house, she asked the driver to stop. She jumped out in utter joy and ran to a woman who was standing at the entrance to the house shouting "Mother, mother." The girl took the woman's hand and led her straight to her (the girl's) bedroom. The girl was able to point out all her toys and all her clothes. It turns out that this woman had a daughter who

passed away many years before. This girl was able to remember details that only the girl who passed away could have known. The girl's current parents were shocked at this display of memory and took a while before they could get used to the fact that their daughter is a reincarnation of another girl who passed away years ago.

(Dr. Ian Stevenson, *Children Who Remember Past Lives*)

3. Reincarnation is an ancient, mainstream belief in Judaism. The Zohar, written by Rabbi Shimon bar Yochai close to two thousand years ago, speaks frequently and at length about reincarnation. Onkelos, a righteous convert and authoritative commentator of the same period, explained the verse, "Let Reuben live and not die..." (Deuteronomy 33:6) to mean that Reuben should merit the World to Come directly, and not have to die again as result of being reincarnated. The great Torah scholar, commentator and kabbalist, Nachmanides (Ramban 1195–1270), attributed Job's suffering to reincarnation as hinted in Job's saying "God does all these things twice or three times with a man, to bring back his soul from the pit to...the light of the living."

(Job 33:29,30)

4. Rabbi Chaim Vital explains in detail the Jewish concept of re-incarnation. The soul is placed in a body in order for a person to attain spiritual perfection by refraining from transgression and performing mitzvot. If one accrues too much spiritual damage, the soul must return to repair the damage. Similarly, if one didn't take full advantage of the opportunity to perfect the soul, it may be reincarnated to complete its perfection. The way it works is as follows:

The first time a soul enters this world, the person is able to perfect the three lower levels of soul: nefesh, ruach, and neshama. If so, the soul goes to "the world of souls" where it awaits resurrection. If not, the different levels of soul can only be perfected in different lifetimes. Each time a level of soul is perfected, the person dies, is reincarnated, and given the chance to perfect the next level of soul. Previously perfected levels of soul are not damaged by sins in the current reincarnation. The soul continues to be perfected in this way until it is perfected at least in nefesh, ruach, and neshama, at which point the soul goes to "the world of souls." The bodies of all the soul's reincarnations will be resurrected, but the first body is the main one.

Another reason souls may be reincarnated is for *zivug* (soulmates): Either because they missed their zivug, and perfection can only be achieved through marrying one's soul-mate; or even if they married but one soul wasn't perfected, the other must return to be with its zivug. Sometimes even a perfected soul, such as that of a tzaddik, may be reincarnated in order to help perfect others. While a person is not aware of previous reincarnations, the Arizal explained that those areas of Torah that a person particularly enjoys learning are those that weren't completed in previous lives and should be concentrated on now. Conversely, the mitzvot that one finds particularly difficult are specifically those needing correction.

The majority of kabbalists are of the opinion that in addition to the first life, there are at most three incarnations. They cite the above-mentioned verse from Job "twice or three times with a man...." The Zohar says this on the verse "punishing the iniquity...to the third and fourth generation [reckoning from the first life]" (Exodus 34:7). However, Sefer HaBahir says that a soul can be reincarnated a thousand times. The renowned kabbalist of the 1600s, Rabbi Menashe ben Israel, resolves this contradiction by saying that since the purpose of reincarnation is to perfect the soul, after three times with no progress the soul loses its chance ("three strikes and you're out"). But if the soul is progressing, even in small increments, it can be reincarnated many times. Another resolution is that the soul can be reincarnated as a human only three times, as suggested by the verse "twice or three times with a *man*." Afterwards the soul may be reincarnated even a thousand times as a lower life form.

The following story illustrates how past wrongs may be corrected through reincarnation:

> Once, a poor man complained to the Ba'al Shem Tov about his suffering. The rabbi sent him to a certain man in a distant town that might be able to help him. When he arrived and asked directions to the man's house, one person after another spat and cursed at the mention of his name. Finally he reached the house only to have the door slammed in his face. After pleading with the owner of the house for an explanation, he was told that the man he wants, a terrible miser hated by all, died long ago. Bewildered, the man returned to the Baal Shem Tov and told him what happened. The rabbi looked him square in the eyes and said: "The man you were looking for was you!" The man realized the reason for his poverty, and started giving whatever he had to charity. Eventually he was able to give extensively.
>
> (Ohr Somayach, Ask the Rabbi website)

5. Consider the implications of the idea of the Fon, a sect of the Benin Republic of Africa. According to them, if I were to die now, a whole fraternity of people and creatures – birds, foxes, lions, fish, men, women, babies, grandmothers, streams, clouds, insects, flowers, and trees – according to their own life schedules, would die with me. And because we died together, we would return together. Though we may be strangers, unknown to each other, we form a cohesive group, and that very group affords us the security of belonging.

(Dr. Sukie Miller, *After Death*)

6. In Nigeria, I was once invited to an elegant meal at the home of a well-known professor. "Ah, here comes Father," the man announced…and we all stood up, expecting, judging from the professor's age, a frail old man in his eighties. Into the room scampered a three-year old, full of energy and curiosity. My host,

noticing my confusion, showed me a mark on his son's forehead and explained that his father had had the very same mark in the same place. "He is part of all our family meetings, all our decision making, sitting where my father sat. He *is* my father...The return of the spirits is a reality...they leave and they return. It is a cycle."

(Dr. Sukie Miller)

7. Among a particular group of Australian Aborigines clouds are the medium for the passage of spirits. When spirits are released from the body at death, they rise up from the ground as clouds and drift across the sky until they come down again as rain. The rainwater enters the watercourses and rivers, and the spirits within it become part of rocks that surround people's wells and the sacred objects that the people place at the bottom of those wells. Without their knowledge, women who pump, wash in, or drink the water, conceive – that is, the spirits in the water, wells, and rocks, enter their bodies as new children. In this way, spirits once housed in living bodies on earth become reborn into others.

(Dr. Sukie Miller)

8. It is a rare culture in which death is utterly final and the human spirit is obliterated with no promise of a return...To admit the possibility of rebirth and return is to step away from fear.

(Dr. Sukie Miller)

9. An evolving body of Jewish folk wisdom has come to us and this material is often funny and sweet. This small tale, suitable as a child's bedtime story, takes rebirth for granted and treats its mysteries with a light shrug.

People wonder: If we have lived before, why don't we naturally remember?

People wonder: If we have been in Heaven, why don't we naturally remember?

People wonder: If we have all lived and died before, why don't we naturally remember?

The answer is simple.

Go to the mirror and look at your face, particularly at the space between your nose and lips.

See the little dent? It was made by the archangel Gabriel.

When he sends us from Heaven into life, he puts his finger right under our noses. He makes that little dent to remind us of what he tells us: "Shhhhh," he says, "Where you've been is a secret. Don't tell!"

The above story is familiar to many observant Jews in the context of when a Jewish baby is in the womb, it is taught the entire Torah. Before the baby is born, he is tapped on the area above the mouth during which he/she forgets what was learned. A reason for this is in order to be able to labor at learning Torah in this world, which has its many rewards.

Chapter Five

Inspiration

1. During illness, the quiet way of being…flows from one's center. It is focused, authentic, genuine, and accepting of any outcome. It is not self-conscious and contains no pity for the "I" who is sick. It is not contaminated by fear of death, and contains no blame or guilt. It does not exclude any therapeutic approach, and may involve using drugs or surgery as naturally as contemplation, meditation, or prayer. It is unconcerned with tragic outcomes, even death, for it rests in the understanding that one's higher Self is immortal and eternal, and cannot die.

(Dr. Larry Dossey, *Healing Words*)

2. If we allow ourselves to enter the quiet, still place of prayerfulness, we can understand the co-relationship of health and illness in the natural order; we can sense how John Updike could say, with wide-eyed astonishment and gratitude, "We do survive every moment, after all, except for the last one." Prayerfulness allows us to reach a plane of experience where illness can be experienced

as a natural part of life, and where its acceptance transcends passivity. If the disease disappears, we are grateful; if it remains, that too is reason for gratitude.

(Dr. Larry Dossey)

3. Almost in tears from pain, I limped a few kilometers with our long column of men from the camp to our work site. Very cold, bitter winds struck us. I kept thinking of the endless little problems of our miserable life. What would there be to eat tonight? If a piece of sausage came as extra ration, should I exchange it for a piece of bread? Should I trade my last cigarette, which was left from a bonus I received a fortnight ago, for a bowl of soup? How could I get a piece of wire to replace the fragment which served as one of my shoelaces? Would I get to our work site in time to join my usual working party, or would I have to join another, which might have a brutal foreman?.... I became disgusted with the state of affairs which compelled me, daily and hourly, to think of only such trivial things. I forced my thoughts to turn to another subject. Suddenly, I saw myself standing on the platform of a well-lit, warm, and pleasant lecture room. In front of me sat an attentive audience on comfortable upholstered seats. I was giving a lecture on the psychology of the concentration camp! All that oppressed me at that moment became objective, seen and described from the remote viewpoint of science. By this method I succeeded somehow in rising above the situation, above the sufferings of the moment....

(Viktor Frankl, *Man's Search for Meaning*)

4. Ten months after the tragic bus accident in Israel that left our dear son-in-law in a coma, on the ninth day of Kislev, Rabbi Eliezer Geldzahler passed away. Notwithstanding the unprecedented volume of vigils, prayers, supplications, importuning and acts of charity, kindness and piety worldwide dedicated to his recovery, the response of the Master of the Universe, our Heavenly Parent, was "no."

From the depth of our collective pain comes the inevitable question, "Are we to understand that our prayers were in vain? That the never ceasing recitals of Psalms of our devoted friends everywhere were for naught?"

One of Reb Eliezer's students related a parable of two fathers who enter a clothing store to purchase garments for their family. One is very specific about the requirements, i.e. style, size etc. The other moves through the store quickly, choosing one suit after another. When asked for an explanation about their different approaches, it came to light that the former had only one child to clothe and had to make sure that the suit was perfect for him. But the latter had a house full of children and figured that if a garment wasn't quite right for one, it would undoubtedly fit another one of his children.

Similarly, the Almighty has many beloved children. For some unfathomable reason that only He knows, our prayers could not fit or work for Reb Eliezer in the way that we had hoped. But without a doubt, the massive, positive, spiritual energy released by our supplications will work for the many others who need them. And hopefully, they will also provide strength for his wife, our daughter Baila, and their 13 beautiful children.

Most certainly these prayers will accompany Reb Eliezer to his eternal abode and be a merit for his soul. Our friends everywhere, who invested heart and soul in their prayers on our behalf, please be assured that we will always be grateful, and that your efforts were not wasted. They are a good fit for someone, somewhere and certainly we and our world are better because of them.

(Rebbetzin Feige Twerski, Milwaukee, wi)

5. The members of Henry's family and all his friends were amazed at the equanimity with which he faced his death. Few of us shared his beliefs and many wondered how on earth these ideas could have arisen in the mind of a New York businessman. But there was no mistaking Henry's curiosity as to what was to happen to

him. At the time of his death, Henry's family was there to witness its indisputable power in the visions it brought him and to give him comfort and ease. At the moment of his death, Henry opened his eyes and said with difficulty, "Oh, am I still here?" When told he was, he responded in a very weak voice, "Where I'm going is so beautiful."

This story (of a past patient) is yet another persuasive argument that death is a threshold rather than a door slammed shut and that the universe is a place of more than meets the eye.

(Dr. Sukie Miller, *After Death – Mapping the Journey*)

6. In Sulawesi, Indonesia when a child dies it is buried in the carved-out trunk of a beautiful tree. As the tree grows, the child is taken closer to the heavens and to God...Into my mind came the prayer flags of Tibet – handmade pieces of colorful cloth inscribed with messages and hung on wires on almost every house. The Tibetans hang these flags around their homes so that the winds will spread the prayers or greetings written on them throughout the world. The tree, I reflected, was doing the same with these children; spreading their spirits into the air around us and who knows where else.

(Dr. Sukie Miller)

7. Dear Seri,

You did not really know me. But I knew you. I am the father of your sister's best friend. For over a year, since your original diagnosis, a lot of people that you hardly knew really, really wanted you to get better. We *davened* (prayed) every day for you, mentioning you in the part of the *shemonah esrei* (prayers) where we ask God to cure the sick. We said *Tehillim* (Psalms), hoping as hard as we could that God would make you better.

While I spend most of my time being a doctor, I spend a lot of time thinking about how Judaism looks at life. I think about why people get sick and wonder what the Almighty wants us to do about all kinds of questions that come up in medicine. Grown-ups call it medical ethics, but it is really nothing more than learning what the Torah has to say about medical problems that people have. It is not so different from the Torah your teacher was teaching your class before you became too sick to go to school.

I also spend time wondering what God is trying to tell us when people get sick. I particularly wonder how He wants us to understand when a five-year-old has to spend her days at the hospital instead of spending time on the playground with her kindergarten friends. People ask me how a life that ends at the age of six can possibly have meaning. I understand why they ask the question and I wonder if you also asked that question during the past year. You may not have understood what was happening, but the rest of us did.

And because we understood what was happening, we changed our lives. You were too little to know that people unfortunately get sick all the time, and sometimes they die. And we are very sad when that happens, but we usually don't do much about it. We mention them in our prayers and we add them to our *mishaberach* lists (the list of sick people who we specially mention in *shul* when we read from the Torah). We hope that they get better, but if they don't, we are sad and we move on.

But when we found out that you were ill, our whole community changed, both the men and the women. We added *Tehillim* groups to say Psalms for your recovery. We learned Torah in your merit. We added special classes on *lashon hara* (the laws of gossip), hoping that if we became better people, maybe you would get better. I do not think you could have understood how hard it is to convince grown ups not to gossip or say mean things about people for just two hours each day, but people thought that it would be worth it if it might help you get better.

We realized that God was sending us a message, so we all starting doing extra mitzvot (commandments), all as a merit for you to get better. As you became sicker, we tried harder. We increased our *chesed* (acts of kindness), dedicated ourselves more to *bikur cholim* (visiting the sick), and gave more *tzedakah* (charity).

In the end, there will be some who will say that all of the extra mitzvot that were done for your sake did not help at all. They will think that it just shows that God did not care. But those of us who lived through the last year knowing how sick you were know better. We know the real answer to the question of how a life of only six years can have meaning.

A rabbi once told me that the value of a particular life might not be apparent to the one who is living that life. There are people who are so sick that they do not know what is happening around them, like what happened to you near the end of your short life. And the rabbi told me that people would say that such a life has no value since the sick person cannot appreciate it. But he also told me that the real value of that life might be in the impact that it has on the people around it. He told me that the increased number of mitzvot done by the people around the sick person may not always be apparent to us, and that we will never know the impact the ill person has had on others.

But that rabbi was not completely right. Now that your life is over, I can see the impact that your life had on others. I do not think that the shul would have cancelled a big event for just anyone's funeral. But who would have shown up at the shul instead of at your funeral anyway? How could all of those hours of Tehillim, learning Torah, and guarding our tongues not leave a permanent, lasting impact on each of us and on our community? Unifying a Jewish community is no easy trick.

So I guess that from now on, when people ask me how any life, even one that is cut tragically short, can possibly have meaning, I will have an answer. The value of a life is not measured in years, but in the impact it has on others. If the accomplishment of a person's purpose in life is calculated by how many individuals it helped to make into better people, then there is only one conclusion to be drawn. Some people live a long time, but don't accomplish much, and some people accomplish a whole life in six years.

Goodbye, Seri.

(Dr. Daniel Eisenberg, www.aish.com)

8. Life is not measured by the amount of breaths we take, but by the moments that take our breath away.

(Author unknown)

9. Michoel Abrahamson was a brilliant and dedicated talmid (student) at the Chofetz Chaim Yeshiva in Queens, NY. After he married, he continued to live in Queens near the Yeshiva. He had a devoted wife, beautiful children and a future full of promise. Then, tragedy struck.

He had terrible stomach pains and was eventually diagnosed with stomach cancer. His condition worsened rapidly and he soon found himself in Sloan-Kettering Hospital in Manhattan, one of the top cancer hospitals in the world.

Moshe Shaps, a friend of his from Yeshiva, used to visit him frequently to help him with his physical and emotional needs. Rabbi Shaps is now the Rosh Yeshiva (Dean) of Yeshiva Tiferes Naftoli in Manalapan, NJ.

Mrs. Chavie Bernson, from the Chofetz Chaim Yeshiva Kollel, knew a nurse, Yehudis Halperin, who worked in Sloan-Kettering. She asked Yehudis to look in on Michoel to help him in any way. Yehudis was not assigned to Michoel's floor but she did visit him frequently. She was a particularly valuable resource because she knew the ins and outs of the hospital and she understood the sensitivities of an observant Jewish patient.

Michoel benefited greatly from Moshe and Yehudis. Rather than lie back and wither away in despondency as if his life were over, it occurred to Michoel that Moshe and Yehudis had something in common – they were both single. The two of them had not met to this point. Michoel was about to embark upon a new career – that of matchmaker.

He broached the subject with each of them. Each was re-luctant. Firstly, Michoel only knew Yehudis very briefly, so how could he know that they would be a suitable match? Secondly, even if they would happen to be compatible, the two of them had very different goals. There was nothing to talk about – or so they thought.

Michoel was undaunted. He told them each individually, about a passage he had read in an Artscroll Maggid book written by Rabbi Paysach Krohn. The Gemora (Shabbos 127a) lists actions through which a person receives reward both in this world and the world-to-come. The following items appear on that list: ...*visiting the sick, arranging for a bride, and escorting the dead*...It seems out of order. *Escorting the dead* should follow *visiting the sick* – that is the logical progression. Why is *arranging for a bride* stuck in there, apparently out of place? The Steipler Rav answered that the merit of *arranging for a bride* is so powerful that it can separate between *visiting the sick* and *escorting the dead*. In other words, if Michoel could arrange this match, it would be a heavenly merit for his health and his very life.

After hearing this, how could either of them say no? They agreed 'under duress' to meet and go on one date. Well guess what. They actually liked each other very much, continued dating, and in due course, got engaged.

A short time later, Michoel had a near-fatal episode. His stomach was bleeding because of the cancer. He was losing blood so rapidly that they could not transfuse the blood into him fast enough. There was no doubt in anyone's mind that Michoel would be gone in a matter of hours. That is, anyone except Michoel. When the Rabbi asked him to say his final confessional (*viduy*), he refused. Saying *viduy* was, to Michoel, a statement that he was giving up on his life.

The entire hospital was stunned that Michoel made it through that fateful day and eventually managed to be released. He could now live at home again with his precious family. What's more,

Michoel, who by all medical logic, should have expired back in the hospital, lived to attend the wedding of Moshe and Yehudis, albeit ravaged with cancer.

Michoel died a few weeks later. He passed away, confident that the mitzvah of *arranging for a bride* and the implicit blessing of the Steipler Rav, extended his life beyond what 'should have been.' Michoel was a young man who, no matter how grim and tormented his situation was, always chose life.

(Shulweek, Oct. 7, 2005)

Chapter Six

Prayer

1. When praying on behalf of those who are seriously ill and they pass on, there is a tendency to grow despondent and to be overcome by a feeling that one's prayers are for naught. The Steipler Gaon once enumerated some areas in which such prayers achieve significant accomplishment:

a. The prayers may very well have diminished the patient's suffering to some degree.

b. The prayers may have extended the patient's life by a few months, weeks, days or even a few hours. Even a moment of life, said the Steipler, is of inestimable value and is more precious than gems.

c. Even if the prayers affected no change at all in the patient's condition, they still are a source of merit for her, since all those who prayed aroused heavenly compassion through their prayers, which were uttered because of her. These merits will stand by her in the World to Come and may also protect her offspring in the future.

d. These prayers can bring salvation to other individuals and to the community as a whole. At the End of Days, when all will be revealed, we will learn how each prayer uttered by each individual brought about great goodness and salvation.

(Rabbi Shimon Finkelman, *More Shabbos Stories*)

2. Someone complained about how thousands around the world said Tehillim for Rabbi Shlomo Zalman Orbach and the prayers did not seem to be answered. I was one of the few people who did not know that the world was praying for Shlomo Zalman ben Rivka (Rabbi Orbach) on that particular Shabbat because at the very same time I was desperately praying for another Shlomo Zalman ben Rivka, my brother, who was in the hospital fighting for his life. In shomaim (heaven) that day, perhaps because of the Tehillim said by so many, it was decided that a Shlomo Zalman ben Rivka must live and recover, and so perhaps it was with that in mind that my brother recovered so well. The world asked that Shlomo Zalman ben Rivka recover, and although many did not know it, that is exactly what happened. We may not know how our prayers are being answered, but know that not one word is ever wasted.

(Moshe A. Handler, "Two Nissim and a Funeral," *The Jewish Interest Magazine* 1995)

3. Following a diagnosis of cancer of the throat, patient X showed no tendency to lapse into depression, despair, lack of motivation, and fear of death, which is typical in many patients. He did not engage in specific prayers in which he pleaded or bargained with God to "change the diagnosis" and grant him a cure. He did not "fight" cancer in any ordinary sense of the word, as doctors and

others often recommend today. His attitude was rather one of renewed commitment and gratitude to God, combined with the belief that God's will was being done, no matter what happened. This patient ended up living for the next 13 years without any form of medical treatment or surgery. Repeated evaluation revealed no evidence of the laryngeal tumor. He eventually died at age 78 from an unrelated cause.

This case demonstrates that often a prayerful, prayer-like attitude of devotion and acceptance – not robust, aggressive prayer for specific outcomes – precedes the cure. Cancers sometimes regress spontaneously, not when some specific formula is followed, but when all formulas are abandoned.

(Dr. Larry Dossey, *Healing Words*)

4. Visualization is used to imply deliberately constructed wordless thoughts directed toward a desired goal. There is a debate over whether goal-free or goal-directed visualizations work best in prayer. The most important realization is that both work. Hence, choose the method that intuitively feels best for you. Highly specific, goal-directed prayers seem unnatural, even arrogant, to many people who may feel it isn't proper to "tell God what to do." Other individuals prefer an aggressive, robust, "make it happen" approach that involves highly specific and goal-oriented prayers and visualizations...Personality factors are undoubtedly involved in these preferences, such as the levels of introversion and extroversion present in one's psyche. These personality traits are extremely resistant to change and tend to be stable across a lifetime. We should acknowledge them for what they are, and take them into account in our personal prayer strategy.

(Porter and Norris)

5. A woman in California was stuck in traffic due to a car accident. She decided to say tehillim for the people in the accident. When the traffic began moving, she passed the scene of the accident and saw a woman lying on the pavement. She said a special prayer

for her and then kept going on her way. A few months later, the lady who said the prayer received a phone call from a woman she did not know. The woman said she was calling to thank her for saving her life. She recounted that she had been in a car accident and was dying. The next thing she remembered was seeing Hebrew letters floating in the air and being greeted by a Being from "the other side." She was told that she was supposed to die, but because of a lady's tehillim and special prayer, her life would be spared. The Being pointed to the lady in the car, and the injured woman looked at the license plate and memorized the number. Upon recovering from her injuries, she traced the license plate and found the telephone number and called the lady to thank her for praying for her.

(A personal communication picked up from
the Har Nof Internet ListServe, Jerusalem)

Chapter Seven

Spiritual

1. Very often a dying person chooses to die when a certain relative gets there, or certain people are in the room, or when they are left alone – even if they are comatose or heavily sedated. This is a special gift to those present. It is often the most spiritual moment in our lives to be with a loved one at the moment of death.

(author unknown)

2. Near death experiences, mystical states, prophesies, answered prayer, visions, out of body experiences, astral travel, reincarnation, life before life, life after life, meditation, metaphysical, spirituality are actual perceptions of a spiritual reality and not mere hallucinations.

(author unknown)

3. Every cloud has a silver lining. Make sure to be in that area of the lining so that the darkness of the cloud does not rain on your party.

(Yehudit Dasberg, Tiferet Gadi Tape Library)

4. As a kid growing up, *yizkor* (memorial service) was a murky and mysterious time. As it approached in the prayer service, our parents would push us out of the room, and we would gladly go. Parent and child alike were relieved and thankful that we knew nothing of what was about to transpire. This was one section of the siddur that we systematically skipped over, blissfully ignorant of its contents. As we would file back in, minutes later, I would see a different congregation than the one I'd left: The women praying around me had been transformed into sobbing statues with blank faces and far-off looks, transported to a world I could barely imagine. What had they experienced; what had they suffered? I didn't have a clue, because hardly a word was ever uttered about yizkor, about what was said or what was done in those few moments while I was away.

And now, here I was on this last day of Pessah, in my fiftieth year, standing shoulder-to-shoulder with my three daughters, reciting yizkor for our beloved Ari. How I wished I could push my own kids out the door! I watched painfully as our youngest, only ten years old, slowly read the short prayer asking God to embrace Ari in the World to Come, and I thought: A ten-year-old doesn't belong here. The unfamiliar text in small print was hard enough to read without having to battle the tears filling my eyes. And then, the dreaded spot in the prayer where the deceased's name is mentioned and his relationship to the reader indicated jumped out at me. My mouth had never uttered a more obscene phrase as I whispered *b'ni* – my son – in that yizkor prayer. My son?!

My heart yearned to be that little girl again, the one who had to be dragged back into services from the shul playground, or from chatting and laughing with girlfriends. Alas, I'm all grown up now, far removed – altogether too far removed – from the protective bubble of the home in which I grew up. Now I am the parent, charged with the responsibility to love and protect my family with every breath. My son is gone, and here I am, beginning a lifetime of staying in for yizkor. Suspended between life and death, somewhere between this world and the next, I stand there praying, crying, longing for that sweet, smiling little boy with the pure heart and innocent grin, the boy who put an extra NIS 50 in his tzedaka box before every mission. Oh, and if it's not too much to ask, will You give Ari a kiss for me?

(Susie Weiss, "My First Yizkor,"
TeaneckIsrael@yahoogroups.com, April 2004)

5. The reason for the disproportionate number of Down Syndrome children born in Jerusalem is a mystery...Down children are often born in clusters in the same neighborhood or on the same street... A number of unproven theories have been proposed, including the fact that Jerusalem has a high level of electromagnetic radiation in the country from radio and TV antennas, environmental pollution, and heavy metal concentrations in the water. There is also the spiritual perspective, suggesting that Jerusalem is the holiest city and therefore prone to a higher incidence of holy souls coming down in bodies that have no need to keep the mitzvot but are just here to give love.

(*Jerusalem Post*, Friday May 21, 2004)

6. Last week one of my kindness advisors sent me an e-mail link to an article in The New York Times about how medical researchers have found that acts of kindness stimulate the brain in the same place that physical pleasures do. So now medical researchers have shown that doing kindness causes enjoyment. From this you can see one way that I cope with tragedy – I receive tremendous pleasure by promoting kindness.

(Shmuel Greenbaum, TraditionofKindness.org, June 2004)

7. Seeking knowledge, wisdom and truth – collectively, that is what prepares us for the World to Come. We need to be able to peel away the outer layer so that the truth can be revealed. The falsehood of the world needs to be rolled back. Acquiring wisdom in this world equips us to enjoy the existence of the World to Come. The more wisdom we pick up here, the more successful we will be

there. Just as we must prepare ourselves before crossing a street, so too we have to learn how to lead our lives. Lack of preparation is the root cause for all our problems. The next world is real – it is not imaginary. We pass into a gaseous state. This world is transient, temporary. A brief stage in our total existence. God breathed a soul of life into each and every one of us. Whereas the body is here for a brief period, our soul does not cease to be – it continues to exist after it takes off its overcoat. In the next world, the truth will be revealed to all – so that we could enjoy it and His presence in all its splendor and joy.

(Rabbi Avigdor Miller, audio tape – Tiferet Gadi Tape Library, Jerusalem)

8. Hence, it should be abundantly clear to all – we still have our basic questions, we still hurt terribly and feel an enormous hole in our midst. There will be days where we will not feel like answering phones or socializing. If we appear to be curt or slip away from an invitation or event, please note that this is part and parcel of how we are coping vis-à-vis the greater community. We pray that God gives us strength, perseverance, consistency, and wisdom. We do not know what tomorrow brings – we hope and pray that he grants us all good health, sustenance, and good tidings. Let us take this unknown of a situation and turn it around to believe that there is a better life beyond the one we are in currently. We must utilize every spare minute we are given in order to come closer to Him.

There are those who believe that we were placed here on earth, given life, and can now choose what we would like to do with it – as long as we thank God and do what He asks of us. But the life that we get is also intrinsically connected to a spiritual element. We are all messengers in order to complete some sort of task. It is very easy to become utterly disappointed if we think that God has no right to meddle into our affairs especially when we are following His will already. If we don't get what we want when we want it or if somebody or something is taken from us, our natural tendency is to get angry.

There is a story of a person who was invited by his friend to a formal party and was asked to wear a tuxedo and come on time. The friend arrived on time as he was asked to do, but quickly found out that he was invited to the party as a waiter. Naturally, the friend got upset and claimed that had he known ahead of time that he was to be a waiter, he would have welcomed the task and performed it happily, and only afterwards partake in food and drink.

We arrive in this world with the pre-conditioned thought that we're here to have fun, period. Things happen every day that are unexpected. If we plan ahead to serve rather than to take, then the chances of dealing with unexpected challenges successfully are far greater.

There are many souls who aimlessly float around in the heavens who have yet to accomplish their objectives in this world. The Creator gives them additional chances in order to do their tikkun. I would venture to say that there are souls sitting here among us who have already been in the next world and have returned here for one purpose or another. Therefore, we must take advantage of the time given to us here in order to prepare our house for the next world. May we all merit climbing ever higher on the spiritual ladder in bliss under the protective wings of our Creator.

(Author's communication)

9. The next thing I knew...I was standing in a mist, and I knew immediately that I had died...The mist started being infiltrated with enormous light, and the light just got brighter and brighter and brighter, and it is so bright but it doesn't hurt your eyes, but it's brighter than anything you've ever encountered in your whole life.

At that point, I had no consciousness anymore of having a body. It was just pure consciousness. And this enormously bright light seemed to cradle me. I just seemed to exist in it and be a part of it and be nurtured by it, and the feeling just became more and more and more ecstatic and glorious and perfect. And everything about it was…if you took the one thousand best things that ever happened to you in your life and multiplied by a million, maybe you could get close to that feeling. I don't know. But you're just engulfed by it, and you begin to know a lot of things.

I remember I knew that everything, everywhere in the universe was OK, that the plan was perfect. That whatever was happening – the wars, famine, whatever – was OK….

And the whole time I was in that state…I was just an infinite being…knowing that…you're home forever. That you're safe forever. And that everybody else was.

(Dr. Kenneth Ring, *Heading Toward Omega*)

The above parallels a statement in the Talmud: "Better one moment of pleasure in the hereafter than all the pleasures of this world."

(*Pirke Avot* 4:29)

10. While we hear that the "light" in the afterworld is nothing short of magnificent, we as human beings have an opportunity to effect change in ourselves in this world, whereas there in the other world we cannot. One NDEer said "I know that life is for living and that light is for later."

(Dr. Melvin Morse and Paul Perry, *Transformed by the Light*)

11. "Light is sown for the righteous…and will sprout according to how well they cultivated themselves in this life." Hence we should understand that we could do things in this life that have a direct effect on how things will be for us later on.

(Psalms 97:11)

12. A wealthy man was summoned to the palace of the king. In those days, a summons was almost assuredly a bad sign; the person was in trouble with the authorities. It was then that the man found out who his true friends were. Some "friends" immediately

took leave of him upon of the bad news. "You're the one in trouble," they said. "We don't want any part of it."

Others said, "We'll accompany you to the palace. However, we can't go any further. Once we come to the palace gate, we will not be allowed to continue. Sorry."

Thus the man had to enter the palace grounds alone. As he entered the gates, his heart heavy with worry and fear, to his surprise a man was standing at the entrance who said, "I know who you are and why you were summoned." The stranger continued, "Furthermore, I know exactly what needs to be said on your behalf before the king. Have no fear. I will personally escort you into the king's chamber and speak on your behalf, so you have nothing to worry about."

That's what happens when we die, when we are suddenly and unexpectedly summoned to the palace of the King of Kings. The first set of friends, who want no part of us, are our material possessions – our money, our status, our political connections. None of it has any meaning over there. And that's the first thing you realize when you reflect soberly upon your death: how insubstantial over there are the things you considered valuable in this world.

The next set of friends who accompany us to the gate are our family and friends. They arrange the funeral. They accompany the body to the grave. But they can go no further. They're not allowed to proceed with you through the palace gate. And so the person finds himself abandoned again.

There is, however, a stranger waiting at the palace entrance who promises to speak for us in the presence of the King. Who is he, this stranger we do not recognize? He is our good deeds.

(Rabbi Yisrael Meir HaKohen, the Chafetz Chaim)

13. A visitor from London came to meet with Rabbi Yaakov Yisrael Kanievsky (The Steipler Rav), and upon entering his study handed the Rav a note with his name on it. Immediately the Rav asked him if he had a brother living in Bnei Brak. The man said yes. The Rav did not know either brother and invited the brother

to come to his study. They waited a short time until he arrived, and then asked the brother: When you were a young student and had some free time, did you learn at the study hall every Friday afternoon before Shabbat? The brother answered yes. Did you remember, continued the Rav, an old janitor whose job it was to clean the study hall? Yes, said the brother. Did you also remember that this janitor used to interrupt your learning by telling you to move from one place to another in order so that he could clean? Yes, the brother said.

Well, last night this old janitor, who had since passed away, came to me and told me that in his new spiritual world he doesn't feel comfortable because he is bothered by the fact that he caused you to lose precious moments in learning Torah. I am therefore asking you to please go to this man's grave and forgive him for what he feels was a transgression. The brother went and did as the Steipler Rav said.

(*Ashkavtei D'Rebbe*, Part 1 p. 187)

14. The unknown is the approach to the sacred, the spiritual, the unnamable, the numinous (spiritually elevated). To honor this dimension is to be healed. The approach to the numinous is the real therapy and inasmuch as you attain to the numinous experiences you are released from the curse of pathology. Even the very disease takes on a numinous character.

(Carl Jung, in Yaakov Astor's *Soul Searching*)

15. Life is a riddle – death being part of the solution. Some term death as a secret, since it is hidden away from us. Yet if death is a secret, life is all the more so…The knowledge that man's life on Earth stands in the middle, between past life and future life, and is a preparation for the basic life, opens the door to the solution of this great and fundamental problem.

(Rabbi Yechiel Tucazinsky, *Gesher HaChaim*)

16. To the Jewish Sages of old, death generally led to the direct

experience of God. It certainly was not a blank state of being. Interestingly, throughout The Bible, death is designated by a variety of names, which indicate that the spirit survives death:

a. "Going" – similar to going from one place to another. "I shall go the way from where I shall not return" (Job 16:22); "A generation goes..." (Ecclesiastes 1:4); "Man goes to his eternal home" (Ibid. 12:5).

b. "Coming" – "And you shall come to your fathers in peace" (Genesis 15:15); "You shall come to your grave with a rich harvest, like a full sheaf of corn which comes up in its season." (Job 5:26).

c. "Sleep" – "And they shall sleep a perpetual sleep" (Jeremiah 51:39).

d. "Lying" – "Behold, you will lie down with your fathers" (Deuteronomy 31:16); "And David lay with his fathers" (1 Kings 2:7).

e. "Gathering" – "And he was gathered unto his people" (Genesis 49:33).This refers to the deceased being greeted by friends and relatives when he gets to the end of the tunnel and draws closer to the light, as reported by NDEers.

f. "Leaving" – The departure of the soul resembles the setting of the sun that disappears only in respect of what confronts the eyes: "And the sun rises and sets" (Ecclesiastes 1:5).

g. "Rest" – or at rest. "When his spirit rested" (*Ketubot* 104a). Actually the body is not at rest at all. When body and soul part, the various bodily elements begin to change, to move about to form new compounds, while the spirit rises to higher levels. What is meant here is that the spirit comes to rest among its kind and at its destination. It is no longer involved in the exertion and restlessness known in this world.

(ibid.)

17. Do you think of yourself before your birth? Where have your relatives gone who are no longer in this world? They have gone to the source from which you came before your birth. You are eternal.

(Ramana Maharshi, in Stephen Levine's *Who Dies*)

Chapter Eight

Personal

1. One is not alone with fear of death – it affects many people but most choose not to talk about it.

(author unknown)

2. Once you realize you survived a certain pain, it no longer has any power over you. It is part of you, but not who you are.

(author unknown)

3. You don't have to consciously know the root cause of pain, but you do have to feel it and express it in some way in order to realize you survived it by either screaming, writing, drawing, or creative visualization.

(author unknown)

4. There are six emotional stages of personal loss, as experienced after the death of a loved one: shock and denial; fear and panic; anger; bargaining; depression; and temporary acceptance. Shock

and denial occur almost immediately upon receiving the news. Fear and panic will likely occur within the first few days as you contemplate your situation. Anger can also be immediate – and dangerous if it is lingering and allowed to fester. Not everyone goes through the stage of bargaining, which means you seek some type of supreme intervention where you make mental promises in return for granting your wish (to live longer). Depression may be moderate and cured with a good cry. Or it may be so intense that it inhibits normal functioning and requires medical attention. If your sickness is lengthy, you may experience recurring bouts of depression. Acceptance is a level where you have applied a positive attitude and move forward with an effective strategy. How you move through these stages might be slightly different than described, but what really counts is how you manage each stage and that you keep moving through the process.

(Careerbuilder.com, 2004)

5. Imagine your son is the Vice President of the United States. He's busy doing all kinds of good things, but doesn't have the time to call you. You know he's OK, he does important work where he is. Will you get upset that he doesn't call? Would you cry?

(Yehudit Dasberg, audio tape: "Coping with the help of faith." Binyan Shalem, The Institute for Marriage and Family Affairs, 2003)

6. There are certain feelings that cause our soul and spirit to become foreign to us. For example, sadness, fear, depression, frustration, hate, anxiety, anger, etc. While each of these feelings are legitimate, we do not necessarily have to pay homage to each feeling as they arise. We are to be in control and decide the relative importance of each. It is not as difficult as it seems to be a master over these feelings. It is possible to find the good in everything.

(Yehudit Dasberg)

7. We must come to grips with the many deaths – the "little" deaths

we encounter every day, and the big deaths that mark important passages in our lives – that have marked the landscape of our own particular journey, or we can never truly help another person fully.

(Dr. Elisabeth Kubler-Ross, *On Death and Dying*)

8. Only when you are not afraid to live will you be unafraid to die.

(Dr. Kubler-Ross)

9. God sometimes makes our lives difficult to help us release our (untapped) potential. Such suffering has nothing to do with punishment; it is not a response to anything we have done wrong. Rather we are being pushed to develop our potential. The Midrash (*Yalkut Shimoni Yirmiyahu* 289) compares a Jew to an olive. Just as the olive must be crushed in order to produce olive oil, so our potential is only fully realized under pressure.

(Rabbi Yitzchak Kirzner, *Making Sense of Suffering*)

10. If someone lost a family member in a sudden tragic way such as in a *pigua* (terrorist bombing), that individual was selected by God to experience extreme adversity in order to strengthen the rest of us.

(Rabbi Kirzner)

11. Terminal illness not only affects the dying, it also gives survivors a chance to grow. People who take care of someone who is ill do kind acts that help support the world.

(*Pirkei Avot* 1:2)

12. While many doctors view psychological denial as primitive, denial unquestionably helps sick people live longer. Integrating spirituality with psychological defenses can help people live longer as they grow in their relationship with God.

(Dr. Lisa Aiken, *Why Me, God?*)

13. Many dying people would like to talk about death but don't because it makes most listeners uncomfortable. While you can't prevent people from dying, you can be enormously helpful by letting them share their regrets, fears, unrealized dreams, and so on. It is very comforting to know that they don't have to face their fears alone.

(Dr. Aiken)

14. There are some odd things about human dying, anyway, that don't fit at all with the notion of agony at the end. People who almost die but don't, and then recover to describe the experience, never mention anguish or pain, or even despair; to the contrary they recall a strange, unfamiliar feeling of tranquility and peace. The act of dying seems to be associated with some other event, perhaps pharmacologic, that transforms it into something quite different from what most of us are brought up to anticipate… Something is probably going on that we don't yet know about.

(Lewis Thomas, M.D. former President, Sloan-Kettering Cancer Institute, in the *New England Journal of Medicine*, June 1977; as quoted in Dr. Michael Sabom's *Recollections of Death*)

15. When new attitudes regarding death and the "hereafter" were integrated into the lives of individuals such as the case above, a new fervor for day-to-day living was often apparent. For the terminally ill or dying, the effect was usually to focus attention on living for the here and now and away from a preoccupation with death and fear of the unknown. This resulted in a renewed will to live. Another patient of Sabom's said: "I know where I'm headed to, so that I don't have to worry about dying anymore…. I've been through death and it don't bother me. I'm not scared of it. Death is nothing to go through anymore. It's not that hard to die…I know where I'm headed to and I've got my life to live. I enjoy it a lot more."

(Dr. Michael Sabom, *Recollections of Death*)

16. In Judaism it is believed that you are born for a specific event that will occur at some point in your life. But you never know when. You have to always be on your toes, so that when the test comes you will be prepared. It means an opening to a kind of not knowing, to just being. There is nothing you can do to elude any moment but to cultivate an openness to the unknown so that whatever occurs you will be fully present for it. This kind of presence for our life is the perfect preparation for death. It means being open to whatever happens, excluding nothing. Because if everything is OK except death, then eventually you notice that everything is OK except death and loss. And then everything's OK except for death, loss and a bad pastrami sandwich. Then everything's OK except death, loss, a bad pastrami sandwich and the plumber coming. Etcetera.

(Stephen Levine, *Who Dies*)

17. Who is the person who doesn't have the strength to chew the food? Where is that being who had all those social, intellectual and physical identities? You're watching your body get weaker and weaker. You can't take care of the children. You can't earn a living. You can't even go to the bathroom by yourself. Who are you now? For those people who became attached to how it used to be and thought how it always would be, dying is hell. But dying doesn't have to be hell. It can be a remarkable opportunity for spiritual awakening. Instead of tightening into an even greater suffering, they began to let go of the root of their contraction. As their self-image began to melt, they begin to have a little more space in which to experience themselves.

(Levine)

18. It has allowed me to understand why people who were dying and seemed to be having a difficult time often in the last moments went through a considerable change. For some, this "knowing" seems to happen days or sometimes weeks in advance of death. For others, it seemed to happen just moments before they left the

body...At some time, perhaps just a split second before life leaves the body, the perfection of that process is deeply understood...that even those who have held most tightly encounter the perfection and fearlessness of the moment of death.

(Levine)

19. In the movie *Peter Pan*, Captain Hook and Peter Pan discussed how death was the "last great adventure." For most people, however, death is not an adventure, but a terror. There are three main reasons why death is so terrifying to most people: 1) they are afraid of having their sins judged by an Almighty Holy God, 2) they are afraid of the unknown, and 3) they are afraid of the intense pain and suffering sometimes associated with death.

So how do we rid ourselves of this terror?

God promises to be with us even in our darkest hour. He doesn't promise to eliminate the pain and misery, but He promises to be there with us and help us get through the problem. It's important to remember that God does not usually provide us this strength, courage, and grace until we actually need it. He normally provides it on an "as needed" basis.

It's kind of like what happens when you ride a bus. A bus ticket is not usually purchased weeks in advance; you normally purchase it just before you get on. Therefore, don't be discouraged if you don't think you have the courage and strength to handle an upcoming problem. God will provide it when you need it – *if you ask Him*.

A couple days before my dad died, he said, "Tell everyone that it is true; when you walk in the shadow of death, you really don't have to be afraid." Dad exhibited an extraordinary amount of peace his last few days. His life was a testimony that Psalm 23:4 is true. His life showed that even when death is so close to you that its shadow is touching you, there is no need to be afraid; God is with you. You may not see Him, but He is still there. We did not lose my Dad – we were merely separated from him temporarily.

(Michael Bronson, BibleHelp.org)

20. Basic anxiety emerges from a person's endeavors, conscious and unconscious, to cope with the harsh facts of life, the "givens" of existence. Four givens are particularly relevant: the inevitability of death for each of us and for those we love; the freedom to make our lives as we will; our ultimate loneliness; and finally, the absence of any obvious meaning or sense to life. However grim these givens may seem, it is possible to confront the truths of existence and harness their power in the service of personal change and growth.

(Irvin Yalom, M.D., *Love's Executioner*)

21. To adapt to the reality of death, we are endlessly ingenious in devising ways to deny or escape it. When we are young, we deny death with the help of parental reassurances and secular and religious myths; later, we personify it by transforming it into an entity, a monster, a sandman, a demon.... Children experiment with other ways to attenuate death anxiety; they detoxify death by taunting it, challenge it through daredevilry, or desensitize it by exposing themselves, in the reassuring company of peers and warm buttered popcorn, to ghost stories and horror films. As we grow older, we learn to put death out of mind; we distract ourselves; we transform it into something positive (passing on, going home, rejoining God, peace at last); we deny it with sustaining myths; we strive for immortality...by projecting our seed into the future through our children or by embracing a religious system that offers spiritual perpetuation.

(Yalom)

22. Death anxiety surfaces in nightmares. A nightmare is a failed dream, a dream that, by not "handling" anxiety, has failed in its role as the guardian of sleep.

(Yalom)

23. Full awareness of death ripens our wisdom and enriches our life. Many dying patients remark that the most awful thing about

dying is that it must be done alone. Yet, even at the point of death, the willingness of another to be fully present may penetrate the isolation. Even though you're alone in your boat, it is always comforting to see the lights of the other boats bobbing nearby.

(Yalom)

24. I have come to believe that the fear of death is always greatest in those who feel that they have not lived their life fully. A good working formula is: the more unlived life, or unrealized potential, the greater one's death anxiety. When one enters into life more fully, one loses their terror of death – some, not all of it. The *fact* of death may destroy us, but the *idea* of death can save us. In other words, our awareness of death can throw a different perspective on life and incite us to rearrange our priorities.

(Yalom)

25. The attempt to avoid legitimate suffering lies at the root of all emotional illness. Not surprisingly, most psychotherapy patients (and probably most patients, since neurosis is the norm rather than the exception) have a problem, whether they are young or old, in facing the reality of death squarely and clearly. What is surprising is that the psychiatric literature is only beginning to examine the significance of this phenomenon. If we can live with the knowledge that death is our constant companion, traveling on our "left shoulder," then death can become in the words of Don Juan, our "ally," still fearsome but continually a source of wise counsel. With death's counsel, the constant awareness of the limit of our time to live and love, we can always be guided to make the best use of our time and live life to the fullest. But if we are unwilling to fully face the fearsome presence of death on our left shoulder, we deprive ourselves of its counsel and cannot possibly live or love with clarity. When we shy away from death, the ever-changing nature of things, we inevitably shy away from life.

(M. Scott Peck, M.D., *The Road Less Traveled*)

26. In order to live our lives well, we need to believe in a sense and purposefulness of the universe. Even if we cannot find enough evidence to prove it 'beyond a reasonable doubt', we have a need to feel that the cosmos we inhabit is not merely a chance configuration of dead material particles that accidentally give rise to life and mind, but that it is an arena for the evolution of consciousness and spirit – a place where our individual efforts can make a difference toward the realization of some kind of…highest good.

(Gary Doore, *What Survives?*)

Chapter Nine

Cognitive

1. The Almighty does not take anyone up to Him before their time – only upon the completion of their task here, even if it is a passive task. For example, four soldiers are carrying a fifth soldier on a stretcher. If it weren't for the fifth soldier, the other four would not be developing their ability to help others and do good. Likewise, the elderly and disabled give an opportunity for others to do acts of kindness.

(Yehudit Dasberg, Tiferet Gadi Tape Library)

2. Many people do not allow themselves to see the bigger picture. They are seemingly content in their own little world. However, when confronted with certain truths, they either run away or close their minds to it. By remaining open to new information, by making an effort to understand that the pieces of the puzzle aren't all there yet, you allow yourself a measure of serenity and calmness that will promote a healthier lifestyle in this world.

(author unknown)

3. One may think of death like this: Your dream girlfriend doesn't know you exist. You very much exist, just not in her particular consciousness.

(author unknown)

4. In every second of our lives there is an interaction between us and the Almighty. We are all individuals – unique – hence we all have a 1:1 relationship with our Creator. Drastic change can occur in short order, and you never feel deserving of whatever doesn't go the way you want it to. Nonetheless, have absolute faith that everything is for the good – don't worry so much. There is only so much that we ourselves can control. With an ongoing acceptance of the yoke of heaven, we shall thrive in both this world and the World to Come.

(Rabbi Ezriel Tauber, *Ten Steps to Growth*,
Tiferet Gadi Tape Library, Jerusalem)

5. It may seem strange to say it, but we feel quite blessed. Maybe not blessed with healthy kids, but blessed to be allowed to care for God's precious ones that suffer. I am amazed He trusted us with these frail ones and hope I can be the best Mom to them I can possibly be. I would absolutely love a cure, and yet, realistically know it probably is not going to happen in my children's lives. So, with that knowledge, I try to be as positive as possible, even though at times I am afraid and worried. We are all human. We are all mothers (and fathers) who love our kids more than our own lives, and would give our bodies to replace with theirs; taking their pain and trials in a second.

(Darla Klein, mother of several children with
mitochondrial disease, from Mito Internet List, June 2004)

6. Research shows that when you are hateful/angry and vengeful toward others, blood tests show that the lymphocytes (which fight illness) are reduced.

(Miriam Adahan Audio tape, "Twenty-Six
Steps," Tiferet Gadi Tape Library, Jerusalem)

7. Herein lies the secret to feeling that every moment and nuance of one's life has meaning. If you know that not only every action, but every thought and motivation, possesses the potential to fulfill life's purpose, you would not trade the moment for anything; you would be grateful for every moment of life. With such an outlook, even suffering or tragedy – no less than any other life situation – give one the opportunity for choice and therefore have meaning. In fact, adversity offers the greatest opportunity for heroic choice.

(Yaakov Astor, *Soul Searching*)

8. Physical illness, no matter how painful or grotesque, is at some level of secondary importance in the total scheme of our existence. This is the awareness that one's authentic, higher self is completely impervious to the ravages of any physical ailment whatever…The real cure is the realization that at the most essential level, we are all "untouchables" – utterly beyond the ravages of disease and death.

(Dr. Larry Dossey, *Healing Words*)

9. The Ethics of the Fathers (Pirkei Avot) tells us to repent one day before we die. Since we never know when we will leave this world, we should repent every day and live each day as fully as if it were our last (*Shabbat* 153a). Contemplating our last moments of life prepares us to face them when they occur. We can then die with equanimity [calmness, composure] instead of in panic and despair.

(Dr. Lisa Aiken, *Why Me, God?*)

10. Man's fear of death does not only stem from his fear of the transition, but also, and essentially, from his dread of what comes after. This fear also indicates (like every instinct which reveals something of which one is consciously unaware), that man faces a future which he is likely to dread, his having to account for his life. One should, then, be intelligent enough to know that this

temporary life has some purpose. He will accordingly value his life and not allow it to flit by emptily as if he had not lived at all. To recollect this simple and clear fact will not give rise to anxiety, but instead dispels the cares that frequently attend the vanities of this world, the majority of which are worthless, imaginary, and temporary. Relieved of the worries of this world, one frees his mind to engage in purposeful thinking to concentrate upon thoughts that will fill him with spiritual bliss.

(Rabbi Yechiel Tucazinsky, *Gesher HaChaim*)

11. There is an aspect of us – call it "being" or "awareness" or "pure mind" or "I" – that lies behind all the apparent phenomena (our body, emotions, senses, and thinking mind) which appear in the matrix of time and space. We intuit that even when we leave our body at death, this deeper part of our being is unaffected. With this basic change in identity, in the sense of who we are, death is converted from being a frightening enemy, a defeat, an unfortunate error in the universe, into another transformation through which we move, an adventure to surpass all adventures, an opening, an incredible moment of growth, a graduation.

Perhaps this is somewhat analogous to how the early explorers felt after the theory that the world was flat and that one could disappear over its edge was replaced by the spherical concept of our planet. What courage that theory must have released, thus allowing explorers to go fearlessly into the unknown.

(Stephen Levine, *Who Dies*)

12. Before considering what happens after death, just consider what happens in your sleep. Sleep is only the interval between two waking states. Do you survive that interval? The same holds good for death also.

(Ramana Maharshi, in Levine, *Who Dies*)

13. Another way of stating the same idea is: Death is a night that

lies between two days – the day of life on earth and the day of eternal life in the World to Come. We the survivors who do not accompany the deceased on their journey into the night, are left alone staring into the veiled, black void. There is a rage of conflicting emotions that seethes within us: bewilderment and paralysis, agony and numbness, guilt and anger, fear and futility and pain – and also emancipation from care and worry…At the moment of death there is severe disorientation. We are perplexed not only by the large questions of life and death, but by problems of how to feel and how to conduct ourselves properly…And how should we comfort ourselves? Should we appear before family and friends brave, dignified, courageously unruffled? Or may we give vent to our anguish in a stream of tears?…Judaism is a faith that embraces all of life, and death is a part of life. As this faith leads us through moments of joy, so does it guide us through the terrible moments of grief, holding us firm through the complex emotions of mourning, and bidding us (to) turn our gaze from the night of darkness to the daylight of life.

(Rabbi Maurice Lamm, *The Jewish Way in Death and Mourning*)

14. The experiences of [concentration] camp life show that man does have a choice of action…. There were always choices to make. Every day, every hour, offered the opportunity to make a decision, a decision which determined whether you would or would not submit to those powers which threatened to rob you of your very self, your inner freedom….

(Viktor Frankl, *Man's Search for Meaning*)

15. A man who becomes conscious of the responsibility he bears toward a human being who affectionately waits for him, or to an unfinished work, will never be able to throw away his life. He knows the "why" for his existence, and will be able to bear almost any "how."

(Frankl)

16. The concept of "eternity" is a basic building block in the understanding of our lives in this world. The next world has always existed and will always exist. Since our souls (our essence) never die and there is an eternal world, then it follows that our essence always lives. Keeping in mind that there is life after life, the concept of bodily death is merely a tangential technicality to allow the soul to gain entrance to the next world. This transition (what we call death) causes the soul to be elevated.

Because man becomes entrenched in the material offerings that this world contains, his perspective on his ultimate purpose in life becomes clouded and somewhat distorted. Hence, he is more likely to become afraid of all kinds of things. He worries about matters that are beyond his control, which reduces his ability to enjoy life in this world. A person who cries about his future and who is fearful of the unknown is basically acknowledging that he does not believe in an eternal world, and hence, shows of his lack of faith in God.

Those who feel that their fear of death stems from the commitment of sins, would do well to repent – for this is the antidote to reject this fear from within us. However, we must keep our eye on the objective, which is to have a goal in this life. To live our lives defensively takes away from our ultimate goal of fulfilling our purpose here. We must not live our lives here merely to avoid death. We must live our lives to the fullest, because death is but a small chapter along the spectrum of our eternal life.

Having a goal to live a long life is laudable and we should do everything possible to live this life to the fullest in good health and in good spirits. However, the true measure of our lives should be put in the context of its "quality" first, and "quantity" second. If we understand that one of the central reasons we are here is to benefit from the revelation of God's wonder and glory, then our lives begin to take shape and are open to accepting the global perspective – the eternal spectrum that we live in and are constantly experiencing.

(Rabbi Avraham Yitzchak HaCohen Kook, *Orot HaKodesh*)

17. When tragedy befalls us, we should not ask "Why," but "What shall we do now?" It is our choice whether we trivialize our tragedy by crying "Woe is me," or allow it to elevate us, giving our lives new meaning and direction.

> (Esther Wachsman, whose son Nachshon was kidnapped and murdered by Arab terrorists, Jerusalem Post, 2004)

18. The spiritually mindful person seeks to live fully, despite fear, because to allow fear to direct our lives adds the suffering of anticipation to the pain of the loss. No quality is more essential for a well-lived life than courage.

> (Rabbi David J. Wolpe, "Loss is More," in
> Olam Magazine, Winter 1999)

19. The after-life has not been "thought up"; it is not a rational construction of a religious philosophy imposed on believing man. It has sprung from within the hearts of masses of men, a sort of consensus gentium, inside out, a hope beyond and above the rational, a longing for the warm sun of eternity. The after-life is not a theory to be proven logically or demonstrated by rational analysis. It is axiomatic. It is to the soul what oxygen is to the lungs. There is little meaning to life, to God, to man's constant strivings, to all of his achievements, unless there is a world beyond the grave…If the soul is immortal then death cannot be considered a final act. If the life of a soul is to be continued, then death, however bitter, is deprived of its treacherous power of casting mourners into a lifetime of agonizing hopelessness over an irretrievable loss. Terrible though it is, death is a threshold to a new world…

> (Rabbi Maurice Lamm, The Jewish
> Way in Death and Mourning)

20. As we separate and "die" from the womb, only to be born to life, so we separate and die from our world, only to be re-born to life eternal. The exit from the womb is the birth of the body. The exit from the body is the birth of the soul. As the womb requires

a gestation period of nine months, the world requires a residence of seventy or more years. As the womb is a *prozdor,* an anteroom preparatory to life, so our present existence is a *prozdor* to the world beyond.

(Rabbi Lamm)

21. In Mexico, on the annual celebration called the Day of the Dead, the living picnic and even party in graveyards with their dead family members and friends. The ongoing nature of life after death is portrayed with humor and whimsy in the small clay figures of skeletons one sees everywhere. The skeletons – some with eyeglasses, some with hair, some chubby, some thin – are engaged in such mundane tasks as cooking, bathing, putting on makeup, or playing sports...This allows for a kind of familiarity with the otherwise unknown. There is comfort and the potential for strength in the exposure.

(Dr. Sukie Miller, *After Death*)

22. Ask many who fear death what it is precisely that scares them, and the answer is likely to be "the nothingness, the emptiness of it all." Yet no religious or cultural system on earth describes the afterdeath as an amorphous blob, a nothing. Quite the opposite: These systems acknowledge and mitigate the disorienting, anxiety-producing effect of emptiness by rendering in more or less detail a definite *place* beyond death, complete with landscape, inhabitants, climate, colors, routes through it, its own pleasures and dangers...in short, the very opposite of the sudden nothingness that haunts those who fear there is no "more." The systems vary as greatly as belief systems vary on this side of the border, but in no case is the afterdeath vague.

(Dr. Miller)

23. Think of a tree, a living system. A fruit on that tree is part of the system, and when the fruit is ripe, it's at its fullest – flavor, taste, nutritional value; it is ripe to feed. And therefore, it is ready

to leave the system of the living tree to serve the life around it. A patient who is ripe to die no longer resists but accepts the truth of his or her dying. Inevitably then, that person takes practical action to "feed" living loved ones with the fruits of his or her life – writes the will, pays the taxes, ties up loose ends of his business, works out problems in the family. But more than that are the benefits to the dying person of stepping fully into the truth: strife ends when truth prevails; one need no longer struggle. To resist truth is pain; to accept it is to enter seamlessly into reality. Many people suppress the knowledge of impending death out of fear of dying in the here-and-now and fear of harsh judgment and punishment after death. But with truth comes the knowledge that the pain is in the resistance, not in the truth. And along with the struggle, fear can disappear as well.

(Dr. Miller)

24. There is no proof for the survival of the soul, only evidence. As in a court of law, the evidence requires analysis and largely hinges on the credibility of the witness. Our openness of the veracity of the accounts rests in significant part on our own experiences with the paranormal. Each piece of paranormal evidence can be interpreted away or minimized. It is only with the accumulation of anecdotes that we may conclude that our soul survives and returns.

(Rabbi Elie Kaplan Spitz, *Does the Soul Survive?*)

25. Judaism affirms the lesson of the children that Dr. Melvin Morse studied, who after their near-death experiences all finished school, were drug-free, did not fear death, and said that they were brought back to this world for a purpose. The purpose of one's life may be profound in its simplicity. In the words of the Ba'al Shem Tov, "A soul may wait for a millennium to descend to earth, and then live a whole lifetime for the one moment when he will be able to do another a favor."

(Rabbi Spitz)

26. For a time he was not on a beach in Florida but in a bright blueness in the presence of loved ones who had deceased. He did not see what worlds waited beyond this one, but he knew beyond all doubt that they existed, and the strangeness of them frightened him but also lifted his heart.

He understood that eternal life was not an article of faith but a law of the universe as true as any law of physics. The universe is an efficient creation; matter becomes energy; energy becomes matter; one form of energy is converted into another form; the balance is forever changing, but the universe is a closed system from which no particle of matter or wave of energy is ever lost. Nature not only loathes waste but forbids it. The human mind and spirit, at their noblest, can transform the human condition, lifting ourselves from a state of primal fear, when we dwelled in caves and shuddered at the sight of the moon, to a position from which we can contemplate eternity and hope to understand the works of God. Light cannot change itself into stone by an act of will, and stone cannot build itself into temples. Only the human spirit can act with volition and consciously change itself; it is the only thing in all creation that is not entirely at the mercy of forces outside itself, and it is, therefore, the most powerful and valuable form of energy in the universe. For a time, the spirit may become flesh, but when that phase of its existence is at an end, it will be transformed into a disembodied spirit once more.

When he returned from that brightness, from the blue elsewhere, he sat for a while, trembling, eyes closed, burrowed down into this revealed truth. In time he opened his eyes…and he wondered how he could have allowed his anger to prevent him from seeing others as they truly are – a shining light, all but blinding in their brightness – as are we all.

(Rabbi Spitz)

27. Harav Aharon Feldman, Rosh Yeshiva of Ner Israel paid a *shiva* call and mentioned the following words of chizzuk to the family based on a verse from Shmuel II 12:23: For a parent to lose

a child is painful, to say the least; however, know that you'll meet up again with your child in the future. The separation is only a temporary one.

(Rabbi Hanoch Teller, personal communication)

Chapter Ten

More Inspiration

1. In Gan Eden there are lower and upper sections, each one comprising seven chambers. Every righteous person is given a dwelling place in the World to Come according to his or her merit, and this is like a king with his servants entering a city. They all enter through one gate, but when night comes, every man is given a room in accordance with his rank.

(*Shabbat* 152a)

2. A wealthy man visited the holy Chofetz Chaim, who lived in the barest of homes. 'Where are your grand possessions?' he asked, shocked that such an eminent Rav would live like that. 'Where are *yours*?' the Rav asked back. 'Me? I'm just passing through,' answered the visitor. 'So am I,' the Chofetz Chaim concluded.

(Excerpt taken from *Mishpacha Magazine* [March 22, 2006]: p. 45)

3. Soon after our forefather Yaakov (Jacob) descended to Egypt

to commence the first Jewish national exile, he met the Pharaoh. "And Pharaoh said to Yaakov, 'How many are the days of the years of your life?' And Yaakov said to Pharaoh, 'The days of the years of my sojourns have been one hundred and thirty years; few and bad have been the days of the years of my life, and they have not reached the days of the years of the lives of my forefathers in the days of their sojourns.'" (Genesis 47:8–9) The Kli Yakar explains that Pharaoh inquired about Yaakov's age because he had heard that when Yaakov came to the Nile River the waters rose to his feet. Pharaoh hoped that Yaakov's presence could bring an end to the famine they were experiencing. When he saw how old Yaakov appeared he was concerned that Yaakov was nearing the end of his days. Indeed, his appearance was not an accurate indication of his age, since he aged prematurely because of the unusual amount of suffering he had endured. Despite the legitimacy of Yaakov's point – his life was genuinely difficult – the Midrash says that someone who had forged such an intense relationship with the Divine as had Yaakov should have appreciated the Divine lovingkindness demonstrated when God saved Yaakov from Esav and Lavan and reunited him with Joseph. For one of Yaakov's righteousness and spiritual stature, complaining was inappropriate. Therefore, concludes the Midrash, he was punished by losing a year of life for each word of their conversation. What is perplexing about this Midrash is its statement that Yaakov was punished for Pharaoh's words. Even if Yaakov was expected not to complain, why should he be punished for being asked a question? Rabbi Chaim Shmulevitz explains that Yaakov looked older because he allowed his sorrows in life to affect him. True contentment is not in the fulfillment of what you want, but the realization of how much you already have. Had Yaakov focused to the best of his ability on the great benevolence shown by God, despite his travails, he would not have appeared as aged as he did. This fault led to Pharaoh's inquiry and for this he was punished. A parable is told of a man who discovered that he had won the lottery. As he celebrated he accidentally knocked over and broke a vase. His concern over the broken vase was not so great for he realized he had something much more valuable. We all have gifts from God – vision, hearing, health, loved ones. When we stop and appreciate the value of what we have, we maintain the proper perspective to deal with the difficulties we endure.

(Rabbi Shlomo Jarcaig, http://www.torah. org/learning/kolhakollel/5764/vayigash.html)

4. A mouse looked through a crack in the wall to see the farmer and his wife open a package.

"What food might this contain?" the mouse wondered. He was devastated to discover that it was a mousetrap. Retreating to the farmyard, the mouse proclaimed the warning: "There is a mousetrap in the house! There is a mousetrap in the house!"

The chicken clucked and scratched, raised her head and said, "Mr. Mouse, I can tell this is a grave concern to you, but it is of no consequence to me. I cannot be bothered by it." The mouse turned to the pig and told him, "There is a mousetrap in the house! There is a mousetrap in the house!" The pig sympathized, but said, "I am so very sorry, Mr. Mouse, but there is nothing I can do about it but pray. Be assured you are in my prayers." The mouse turned to the cow and said "There is a mousetrap in the house! There is a mousetrap in the house!" The cow said, "Wow, Mr. Mouse. I'm sorry for you, but it's no skin off my nose." So, the mouse returned to the house, head down and dejected, to face the farmer's mousetrap alone. That very night a sound was heard throughout the house – like the sound of a mousetrap catching its prey. The farmer's wife rushed to see what was caught. In the darkness, she did not see it was a venomous snake whose tail the trap had caught. The snake bit the farmer's wife. The farmer rushed her to the hospital, and she returned home with a fever. Everyone knows you treat a fever with fresh chicken soup, so the farmer took his hatchet to the farmyard for the soup's main ingredient.

But his wife's sickness continued, so friends and neighbours came to sit with her around the clock. To feed them, the farmer butchered the pig. The farmer's wife did not get well; she died. So many people came for her funeral, the farmer had the cow slaughtered to provide enough meat for all of them.

The mouse looked upon it all from his crack in the wall with great sadness.

So, the next time you hear someone is facing a problem and think it doesn't concern you, remember – when one of us is threatened, we are all at risk. We are all involved in this journey called life. We must keep an eye out for one another and make an extra effort to encourage one another. Remember, each of us is a vital thread in another person's tapestry; our lives are woven together for a reason.

(Author unknown)

5. Dvar Torah: The Notebook

In 1991, our three-month-old son, Shlomo Moshe Lederman, returned his soul to his creator. While we were sitting shiva, a number of Rabbis offered words of consolation. I found these words very inspiring. I wrote them down in a notebook (not a laptop, an actual paper notebook). I have never shared the contents of this notebook publicly. I do so now in honor of the occasion of the second yahrtzeit of Hindy Cohen, a"h.

a. The Rosh Yeshivah, Rabbeinu HoRav Henoch Leibowitz *shlit"a*, told me that after Avraham was finished eulogizing Sarah, the Torah writes, "*Vayakam me'al pnei maiso.*" "He arose from before his dead (wife)." The word *vayakam* is *mashma* (implies) he arose very abruptly. The Rosh Yeshivah explained that Avraham was in the middle of his eulogy for Sarah when he heard a voice in his head say: 'It was your fault that she died.' Immediately he withdrew, stopped his eulogy, got up and left. He did this because he realized that the voice of guilt was a *maaseh satan* (act of *satan*), and the only way to fight the *satan* was to be *mistalek* (withdraw).

One thing we noticed is that we had enormous feelings of

guilt, more than was rationally warranted. It was literally like someone opened up a fire hydrant into my brain and thoughts of guilt were flowing in. Other bereaved parents have described similar feelings to me. The Rosh Yeshivah's *vort* (word) was extremely helpful to me because it made me realize that the guilt was unfounded and should be dismissed immediately.

b. Rabbi Dovid Chait told me that *Shir Hashirim* (Song of Songs) depicts the scene of a man walking through the garden, picking figs. This is an allegory for death, meaning that Hashem picks the neshamos from Earth to go with him to Gan Eden. The reason Shlomo Hamelech used a fig for this parable, as opposed to any other fruit, is because a fig has the characteristic that it is very difficult to tell by looking at the outside, when it is ripe. So, too, we cannot tell by looking, which neshamos are ripe to go to Gan Eden. Some take 120 years, some take 60 years, some take 20 years. Our son's *neshama* was 'ripe to be picked' after 3 months.

c. Reb Mayer Pasternack told me in the name of his rebbe, Rav Yaakov Weinberg z"l, that Dovid Hamelech (King David) was supposed to die as an infant. He only lived thanks to Adam HaRishon's intervention. Adam was informed that Dovid was fated to die as an infant, so he took seventy years from his life and gave them to Dovid so that he might live. Dovid's father Yishai was one of four people who had no *aveiros* (sins); yet his infant son would have died (had it not been for Adam's involvement). Therefore you cannot say that *aveiros* caused the death (albeit in this case potential death) – he had no *aveiros*. A parent will often think that it must have been his sins that caused the death of the child. We see from here that that suspicion is unfounded.

d. HoRav Dovid Feinstein *shlit"a* told us that when an innocent dies, it is a *kapora* (atonement) for *Klal Yisroel* (the

Jewish people) and has nothing to do with the parents. Since a baby has no *daas* (knowledge), it is innocent by default. The only fault a baby could have is that it cries and is *mitzta'er* (anguishes) the parents – but a baby cannot help doing so. After hearing Rav Feinstein's *vort* we understood that our baby was a *neshama tehora* (pure soul) chosen to be a kapora for *klal Yisrael*.

Rabbi Elimelech Bluth added later that the Chofetz Chaim said that if a person dies inexplicably (as was the case with our baby) it is a kapora for *klal Yisrael* and has nothing to do with anyone's *aveiros*.

e. The Rosh Yeshiva said that each neshama that comes down to this earth has a mission. Our son's mission was accomplished in 3 months and 3 days, at which point he was ready for Gan Eden. We were *zocheh* (meritorious) to be the vehicle through which he made it to Gan Eden* and going to Gan Eden is a *zechus gamor* (total benefit). There is a rule, *megalgelin zechus al y'dei zakau'in* (good things only happen through good people). So we see, we must be *zakau'in*, otherwise the *zechus* couldn't have come through us.

*Pretty much everyone told us that when an infant dies, he and she goes straight to Gan Eden. Rabbi Siff told us that Rabbi Moshe Feinstein *poskined* (ruled) not to say *kaddish* for infants because they go straight to Gan Eden and don't need our *kaddish* for additional merit.

f. Rabbi Dovid Weinberger told us: When Amram, the future father of Moshe, saw that Jewish baby boys were being thrown into the Nile, he decreed that all Jews should divorce so that babies wouldn't be born. Hence, no baby boys would be thrown in the Nile. Miriam had three objections, including the argument that Paroah's edict was depriving the boys of *olam hazeh* (this world) by throwing them into the Nile, but that her father is depriving them of *olam hazeh* and *olam haba* (this world and the next world). As they will not be born into this world, they cannot continue on to the next world. An *Acharon* asked what was Miriam thinking. Is it worth it to have kids just to have them thrown in the Nile? The answer is a resounding YES!!! We see clearly from here that the *daas Torah* is that if someone could come to you and offer the choice of having a baby and losing him, or, not having him at all, the clear-cut choice is to have him because the only way that poor little neshama can get to *olam haba* is to come down through this earth. Even a miscarriage goes to *olam haba*. You are doing that neshama a tremendous favor.

g. The Rosh Yeshiva told me that the Maharshal asks a *kasha* (difficulty): Yaakov should have realized that Yosef was still alive because there is a *klal* (rule) – *mais nishtachach min halev* (the pain of a deceased loved one becomes forgotten from the heart after a year or so). The fact that Yaakov was *nisabel* (in mourning) for 22 years meant *Yosef lo mais* (Yosef didn't die). The Maharshal answers that when a person is in *tzaar* (anguish), he doesn't realize that he is in *tzaar*. Yaakov didn't think he was in *tzaar*. If you would approach Yaakov he would tell you, "You think this is *tzaar*?! This is nothing! Real *tzaar* is beyond." Usually, as you start feeling stronger you start crying less. Then you feel guilty that you don't love the baby because you're not crying enough. You start to feel that you don't miss the baby enough. The fact that you feel guilty is really proof that you love the child because you don't feel this way concerning other children. The fact is, you are in extreme *tzaar*; you just fail to realize it.

h. The Rosh Yeshiva told me: The brothers came back from *Mitzrayim* (Egypt) and told Yaakov that they were required by the Egyptian ruler to bring their baby brother Binyamin back to *Mitzrayim* with them in order to free the brother who was imprisoned there. Yaakov didn't want Binyamin to travel to Mitzrayim, lest there be an *ason* (tragedy). The Torah says *ason* twice, indicating two tragedies. The *pshat* (explanation) is Binyamin was Yaakov's last link to Yosef. Losing Binyamin would be losing Binyamin and Yosef. The Rosh Yeshiva's father died first. He told me that when he lost his mother it was like he lost his mother and his father.

(Rabbi Baruch Lederman, *Shulweek*, Feb. 24, 2006)

6. When I was quite young, my father had one of the first telephones in our neighborhood. I discovered that somewhere inside the wonderful device lived an amazing person – her name was "Information Please" and there was nothing she did not know. "Information Please" could supply anybody's number and the correct time.

My first personal experience with this genie-in-the-bottle came one day while my mother was visiting a neighbor. Amusing myself at the tool bench in the basement, I whacked my finger with a hammer.

The telephone! Quickly, I ran for the footstool in the parlor and dragged it to the landing. Climbing up, I unhooked the receiver in the parlor and held it to my ear. "Information Please," I said into the mouthpiece just above my head. A click or two and a small clear voice spoke into my ear. "Information."

"I hurt my finger..." I wailed into the phone. The tears came readily enough now that I had an audience. "Isn't your mother home?" came the question. "Nobody's home but me." I blubbered.

"Are you bleeding?"

"No," I replied. "I hit my finger with the hammer and it hurts."

"Can you open your icebox?" she asked. I said I could. "Then chip off a little piece of ice and hold it to your finger," said the voice.

After that, I called "Information Please" for everything. I asked her how to spell 'fix.' I asked her for help with my geography and she told me where Philadelphia was. She helped me with my math. She told me my pet chipmunk that I had caught in the park just the day before would eat fruits and nuts. Then, there was the time Petey, our pet canary died. I called "Information Please" and told her the sad story. She listened, then said the usual things grown-ups say to soothe a child. But I was un-consoled. I asked her, "Why is it that birds should sing so beautifully and bring joy to all families, only to end up as a heap of feathers on the bottom of a cage?"

She must have sensed my deep concern, for she said quietly, "Paul, always remember that there are other worlds to sing in." Somehow I felt better.

All this took place in a small town in the Pacific Northwest. When I was 9 years old, we moved across the country to Boston. As I grew into my teens, the memories of those childhood conversations never really left me. Often, in moments of doubt and perplexity I would recall the serene sense of security I had then. I appreciated now how patient, understanding, and kind she was to have spent her time on a little boy.

A few years later, on my way west to college, my plane put down in Seattle. I had about half an hour or so between planes. I spent fifteen minutes or so, on the phone with my sister, who lived there now. Then, without thinking what I was doing, I dialed my hometown operator and said, "Information, Please."

Miraculously, I heard the small, clear voice I knew so well, "Information." I hadn't planned this but I heard myself saying, "Could you please tell me how to spell 'fix'?"

There was a long pause. Then came the soft spoken answer, "I guess your finger must have healed by now."

I laughed. "So it's really still you," I said. "I wonder if you have any idea how much you meant to me during that time."

"I wonder," she said, "if you know how much your calls meant to me. I used to look forward to your calls." I told her how often I had thought of her over the years and I asked if I could call her again when I came back to visit my sister.

"Please do," she said, "Just ask for Sally."

Three months later I was back in Seattle. A different voice answered "Information." I asked for Sally. "Are you a friend?" she asked. "Yes, a very old friend," I answered.

"I'm sorry to have to tell you this," she said. "Sally had been working part-time the last few years because she was sick. She died five weeks ago."

Before I could hang up she said, "Wait a minute. Is your name Paul?"

"Yes."

"Well, Sally left a message for you. She wrote it down in case you called. Let me read it to you. The note says, 'Tell him I still say there are other worlds to sing in. He'll know what I mean.'"

(Shulweek, March 1, 2006)

7. A man was sleeping at night in his cabin when suddenly Hashem appeared and told the man He had work for him to do and showed him a large rock in front of his cabin. Hashem explained that the man was to push against the rock with all his might. So, this the man did, day after day. For many years he toiled from sun up to sun down, his shoulders set squarely against the cold, massive surface of the unmoving rock, pushing with all of his might. Each night the man returned to his cabin sore and worn out, feeling that his whole day had been spent in vain. Since the man was showing discouragement, the Satan, decided to enter the picture by placing thoughts into the weary mind: "You have been pushing against that rock for a long time, and it hasn't moved."

Thus, he gave the man the impression that the task was impossible and that he was a failure. These thoughts discouraged and disheartened the man. Satan said, "Why kill yourself over this? Just put in your time, giving just the minimum effort, and that will be good enough." That's what the weary man planned to do, but decided to make it a matter of prayer first and to take his troubled thoughts to the Lord.

"Hashem," he said, "I have labored long and hard in your

service, putting all my strength to do that which you have asked. Yet, after all this time, I have not even budged that rock by half a millimeter. What is wrong? Why am I failing?"

Hashem responded compassionately, "My friend, when I asked you to serve Me and you accepted, I told you that your task was to push against the rock with all of your strength, which you have done. Never once did I mention to you that I expected you to move it. Your task was to push. And now you come to Me with your strength spent, thinking that you have failed. Is that really so? Look at yourself. Your arms are strong and muscled, your back sinewy and brown; your hands are callused from constant pressure, your legs have become massive and hard. Through opposition you have grown much, and your abilities now surpass that which you used to have. True, you haven't moved the rock. But your calling was to be obedient and to push and to exercise your faith and trust in My wisdom. That you have done. Now I, my friend, will move the rock."

(*Shulweek*, March 24, 2006)

8. This letter was written by a 16-year old after he was notified that he contracted a terminal illness and wouldn't grace this world further. His last request was that the following be read and internalized as his last will and testament:

"I am quite emotional as I write these words. I know they represent the last memory of me in this world. The world we live in is either just or unjust – you decide.

I just recently turned 16, I am still a child, a baby, in this world...

Yet I managed to love, hate, and fail. On the other hand, I also brought home a grade of 100 that was hung on the kitchen refrigerator with pride, I managed to tell my mother and father "thank you," and also thanks to my closest friend who was there for me through the tougher moments (yes, there were too many). I worked and bought myself a 500-shekel pair of jeans. Yes, I accomplished. I helped an old lady cross the street, went to a concert of my favorite band even though I had to travel way up north in the rain. I beat up a neighborhood bully who always pestered a friend of mine, and I won first place in a competition. I ran into the ocean with friends in the middle of the winter, remained awake all night on the beach gazing at the moon and imagining that there were people who actually walked on it. I even tried once to see how it would feel taking an exam in school without studying whatsoever.

I managed to sit and write this down for you. All of the above I accomplished only after I was told that my life is coming to an end. All of the little things and the bigger ones – I didn't dare do any of them until then. Until then I prevented myself from living life the way I wanted to. I didn't understand what life is all about until that moment when I was told the end is near. Ironically, that is when I started to live.

I don't want to come and say that you should enjoy everything because that is absurd and I know that that is impossible. I also don't want you all to have pity on me and say that life is not fair. It turns out that my best friend is someone else's best friend now, and the 500-shekel jeans really don't fit me well, and when I said "thank you" to my parents, they were busy watching the news, and that meal I had at an expensive restaurant just gave me a stomach ache, and the 100 I got was in an unimportant subject, and the test I didn't study for ended in a failing grade – in math of course, and the concert didn't work out because of a power failure in the middle of the best song, and the TV cameras weren't on me when I won first place.

Nevertheless, all of this! Because I know that I did what I wanted to do. It filled me with the best feeling I ever had. It will have been the last feeling that I merited to feel in this life. Don't bottle up feelings inside – let them out, don't lose perspective, try to stabilize yourself. Don't be embarrassed to tell somebody that you love them because it is the most amazing feeling to be on the receiving end. Use the time that you have for yourself – don't stop and hesitate. I will not forget you – please don't forget me. Take care of yourself. I love you.

Dedicated to all my friends and to all who read these words.

(D. Shoham, who died three days after writing this letter)

PART THREE

Selected Literature Review

Overview

Overcoming the
Fear of Death

There is a vast library of books, journals, articles, movies, Internet sites, and individual accounts detailing aspects of the "deathing" process. Some sources are inspirational, some merely informational. Some follow a regimented theology based on religious practices and beliefs dating back thousands of years, while others include more recent mystical and unexplained phenomena. In reviewing the classical research sources such as *Psychological Abstracts*, *The New York Times Index*, *The Readers' Guide to Periodical Literature*, and *Recent Publications in the Social and Behavioral Sciences*, there were not, relatively speaking, many references under the headings of "overcoming the fear of death," "coping with death," or "fear of death." Perhaps this indicates that, over the years, this issue has been avoided due to the sensitive nature of the subject matter. Despite a more openness over the last 15 years, there are still many who do not wish to put it in the forefront of their thinking, much less write about it.

The fear of death is a universal phenomenon. No matter where one goes in the world, he or she will find large numbers of people who are afraid of dying. The reason for fearing death is because it is the greatest mystery of all (Bronson). Fear of the unknown is highly powerful. Hence, many people, including the religious, find death terrifying. What will it feel like? What will be waiting for us when we reach the other side of the veil of death? Will the afterlife be as chaotic and painful as this life?

Another reason many people find death so terrifying is because we have to face it alone. Even if we have many people surrounding us at the moment of death, we still must pass through it by ourselves. This prospect is very unnerving for many people. Furthermore, the thought of standing before God can be downright terrifying as well. People know that they will have to stand one day before God and give an accounting of their actions. Some people deal with the issue of their mortality by becoming consumed and obsessed with the subject of death. Others simply ignore the subject completely. The only time these people think about death is when they become seriously ill, someone close to them dies, or there is a major calamity. Being obsessed with death is unhealthy and ignoring it can have negative consequences as well. We live in a society conditioned to deny death. It may be for this reason that many, at the time of their dying, feel so confused and guilty. Like sex, death has been whispered about for a long time behind closed doors. The question begs: how can we develop a balanced approach that will allow a person to move on to a less anxious, more positive outlook on life?

This selected literature search surveys a wide range of relevant studies and topics regarding methods used in coping with the fear of death.

Chapter One

Death Anxiety Scales

*I*nvestigators of attitudes toward death have realized the need for standardized measures. Sarnoff and Corwin, Boyar, and Lester ("Experimental and Correlational Studies") have devised measures of the fear of death and investigated the reliability and validity of their measures. However, the items in their scales cover a wide variety of themes; fear of dying, fear of being dead, aversion to funerals, and even worry over the death toll on highways. Does someone who refuses to travel to central Baghdad because he is afraid of being blown up fear death, or is it that he just doesn't want to die *that* way? Many Israelis still sit in cafes in central Tel Aviv – is that a measure of their absence of fear of death?

In a study conducted by Lora-Jean Collett and David Lester ("Fear of Death and the Fear of Dying"), separate measures of death fears were devised in an attempt to distinguish between the fear of death from the fear of the process of dying, and to differentiate between these fears depending upon whether they are for oneself or for another. The sample group they tested showed a significantly higher fear of death than of dying. The low correlations between scores on these scales indicate the potential usefulness of differentiating between these four fears.

Past research designed to investigate people's attitudes toward death and dying has never been able to describe successfully what factors contribute to the personal meaning of death for any one individual. Part of the problem arises from the fact that inter-relationships between fear of death, death anxiety, personality characteristics, and physical well being have never been fully delineated (Robinson & Wood, in Epting, 213). The degree to which an individual has actualized important life goals will influence that individual's fear of death regardless of the degree to which death is integrated into his or her personal construct system. Similarly, an individual's level of integration will significantly influence his or her fear of death regardless of whether the individual is actualized. Moreover, individuals who are highly actualized and highly integrated appear to be significantly less fearful of death and less death anxious than individuals having lower levels of actualization, integration or both. These findings by Robinson and Wood, are associated with healthy adult populations. The research on non-healthy elderly who were closer to death by illness was more concerned and more fearful of death and dying. But contradictory findings reported by several other authors render this matter confusing (214).

Twelker brought together the following cluster of research on age and death anxiety. Some studies have reported that females have higher levels of death anxiety than males (Rigdon & Epting; Thorson & Powell). Some researchers have reported no gender differences (Marks). Servaty et al. reported higher levels of empathy scores for females, and higher levels of empathy were associated with higher levels of death anxiety. Numerous studies have shown inverse relationships of age and death anxiety. Older persons have shown lower levels of death anxiety, and were less afraid of death than younger persons (DePaola, Neimeyer, Lupfer, & Fiedler; DePaola, Neimeyer, & Ross). Gesser et al. explained that young and middle-aged people have a more difficult time accepting the reality of death than do elderly persons. Other studies have shown that religious persons have more positive attitudes toward death than non-religious persons. Alvarado, Templer, Bresler, and Thomas-Dobson found that strong religious conviction was associated with less death anxiety compared to those with weak religious conviction. Fehring, Miller, and Shaw reported that high levels of intrinsic religiosity and spiritual well-being was related to lower levels of negative attitudes concerning death anxiety, as compared with persons with low intrinsic religiosity and spiritual well-being. The findings suggest that religious belief – as expected – plays a part in influencing one's death anxiety. The more religious a person is the less his fear of death; the less religious a person is the greater the fear of death. It was also observed that females, especially older females, had lower mean fear of death scores than males. This finding is not surprising if one would visit many Christian churches, where more females are in attendance than males. Older subjects (age 55–81) did not have higher death anxiety than younger subjects (age 18–25). Although statistically significant differences between age and death anxiety scores were observed, younger subjects had higher death anxiety scores than did the older subjects. As everyone will age, and everyone will die, how people handle the thought of death across the life span is of sociological importance. As people age they experience the loss of friends and families because of death. They learn to cope with the thought of their own death. These findings suggest that older people have resolved the question of death while young people have not resolved the question of death. Death to older people is not as anxiety provoking as it is to young people. It may be that the cognitive awareness of death and death phenomenon creates a feeling of acceptance of death and this is viewed as routine phenomenon (Bond).

Templer concludes, "Death anxiety is usually related more to degree of personality adjustment and subjective state of well-being than to reality factors. Disease has little to do with a respondent's orientation toward death. It may be that any patient diagnosed as having a life-threatening illness who responds with marked fear and apprehension is doing so because he or she has always been very much afraid of death and not because the illness created the fear" (Robinson & Wood).

Chapter Two

Work with Dying Patients

While there are indeed many who prefer not to talk about the subject, it may come as a surprise the extent to which traditional sources such as the Old Testament and the Talmud detail and document cases and stories surrounding the death process. The ancient *Tibetan Book of the Dead* brings to light in the greatest of detail rituals that were common among its people. Different cultures dealt with death in their own ways and practiced what they preached regarding death, especially in the presence of young children, as a natural part of life.

In his psychological commentary to *The Tibetan Book of the Dead*, or the Bardo Thodol, Dr. C.G. Jung describes it as a book of instructions for the dead and dying. Like the Egyptian Book of the Dead, it is meant to be a guide for the dead man during the period of his Bardo existence, symbolically described as an intermediate state of forty-nine days duration between death and rebirth. Lama Anagarika Govinda, in the book's introductory forward, says that indeed, it is the spiritual point of view that makes this book so important for the majority of its readers. If the Bardo Thodol were to be regarded as being based merely upon folklore, or as consisting of religious speculation about death and a hypothetical after-death state, it would be of interest only to anthropologists and students of religion. But the Bardo Thodol is far more. It is a key to the innermost recesses of the human mind, and a guide for initiates, and for those who are seeking the spiritual path of liberation (Evans-Wentz).

Although the Bardo Thodol is at the present time widely used in Tibet as a breviary, and read or recited on the occasion of death – for which reason it has been aptly called "The Tibetan Book of the Dead" – one should not forget that it was originally conceived to serve as a guide not only for the dying and the dead, but for the living as well. And herein lies the justification for having made *The Tibetan Book of the Dead* accessible to a wider public – it has value only for those who practice and realize its teaching during their lifetime (Evans-Wentz).

If the person learns to identify himself with the Eternal, then the fears of death are dissipated. Then he knows that whatever he may see, hear, or feel, in the hour of his departure from this life, is but a reflection of his own conscious and subconscious mental content; and no mind-created illusion can then have power over him if he knows its origin and is able to recognize it. The illusory visions may vary in keeping with the religious or cultural tradition in which the participant has grown up, but their underlying motive-power is the same in all human beings (Evans-Wentz).

This book, however, was intended for Tibetan monks, says Stephen Levine, not for old Jewish ladies dying in Brooklyn! Hence the limitation of its contents are reserved for those people who have incorporated a lifetime of practice into the moment of transition we call death (Levine 272–273).

It may be also worthwhile to note that the teachings described above include much detail about coming into contact with a bright light. The body of the past life will become dimmer and the body of the future will become clearer whereupon this new body shall come upon six lights each representing another part of the next world. The Tibetans teach not to resist the light, but to keep moving towards it in order to prevent being born again. Thus perfect enlightenment is gained. This is just one other indication of the consistency between other reports of a bright light in the Jewish literature and as reported by NDEers (of all religions).

One theory that I once heard (author unknown, n.d.) coincides with another custom reported here that no relatives should weep or make mournful wailings near the dead body. The burial ceremony should rather be a time to celebrate one's passing into another realm – just like we celebrate birthing, we should so celebrate deathing. There is actually a source for this found in the Midrash. When a newborn cries, all the relatives and friends rejoice. When one departs from the world, even if he finds satisfaction in dying, his relatives and friends cry. The first joy and last wail are not connected with what is happening to the person *himself* (his birth or death), but with that which they rejoice in for *themselves*. At his death, they lose a relative and they mourn *their* loss. "When a person is born, all rejoice: when he dies, they all weep. But this shouldn't be so, as we see in the case as described in Midrash Kohelet Rabbah 7:4 of a case of two boats which traverse the ocean, one leaves the port and one arrives back at the port. One may be inclined to be happy for the boat embarking on its voyage as it embraces excitement and adventure, whereas for the one who is returning, nobody is overly exuberant. However, we must look at this situation from the exact opposite vantage point. The boat that is leaving the port is departing to unchartered waters; we do not know what its fate will be, hence that should not be cause for rejoicing. On the other hand, the boat that arrived safely in the harbor should be met with the greatest of joy, now that we know what it accomplished, and that it indeed came back home in peace and in satisfaction. This parable serves as an example of how we ought to look at someone who is about to enter the safe harbor of the next world. Likewise we see that the righteous who were born into this world did not get recognition upon birth (i.e., Moses, his brother Aaron, and Joshua); however, upon death, the world's population was filled with emotion and words of praise and good will.

As we look through the plethora of spiritual literature, the biographies of saints, the death poems that were part of the Zen tradition, the dying of *roshis* with their infinite humor and lightness at death, we see again and again examples of the conscious dying of beings who honor their body but had no remorse at leaving it behind; whose business was finished from moment to moment; who lived their lives… "without leaving a trace" (Levine 260).

Chapter Three

Studies on the Afterlife

Information on the elements of death symbolism was collected from a previous study of 60 societies (Schoenrade). The common theme of the societies was belief in ancestral spirits and reincarnation and their relative positive quality of predicting their afterlife.

Schoenrade explains that afterlife refers to the conditions one's soul must live after death, in the "land of the dead." In some societies afterlife is uniformly pleasant or unpleasant, conditional to a person's behavior while on earth. In other societies, the quality of one's afterlife depends on those still living on earth. For example, the Tlingit of Alaska believe that only when the survivors perform all the mourning rites correctly can a soul be directed to the "land of shadows." Similarly, the Khasi of India believe that the spirit of the dead will go to the "garden of God" if funeral ceremonies are adequately conducted. Thus, the quality of their afterlife is the responsibility of the community at large – it is collective rather than individual.

Consideration of one's personal mortality may be a powerful

source of discomfort. Consequently, the idea that belief in an afterlife reduces the uneasiness linked with the inevitability of death is not new. Berman and Hays postulated that subjects with an initially high belief in the afterlife would view death as having more positive and fewer negative implications, than those who had low belief in afterlife. The subjects consisted of 100 psychology students at the University of Kansas.

For the individuals with positive death perspective, a significant interaction was observed (p < 0.04). Also for negative death perspective, there was a significant interaction (p < 0.003). It seems that when belief in afterlife was strong, a heightened awareness of both positive and negative implications of death occurred. When belief was moderate to weak, the effect of death confrontation on death perspective was dramatically less. The pattern of results on both positive and negative death perspective may be explained in the belief in afterlife as functional for dealing with death.

In an attempt to establish a common linkage between death anxiety and belief in afterlife, Thorson and Powell assessed variables such as respondent sex, race, and religiosity. The results of their study confirm the notion that the belief in afterlife is primarily a function of religion and not, at least directly, a correlate of fear of death. While the study supports the idea that belief in afterlife is inherently a religious concept, it fails to support the notion that the belief in afterlife independently serves the function of reducing death anxiety.

In another study, Kienow and Bolin hypothesized that those respondents believing in a favorable afterlife would show lower fear of death scores. The subjects consisted of 562 people from North Carolina church groups in 1978–79. Virtually all respondents expressing belief in a personal life after death also believed that it would be good for them, independent of denomination preference, frequency of church attendance, or strength of religious belief. Only one person believed her afterlife would be very bad. The authors conclude that the results of this study may be interpreted to indicate that acceptance of the afterlife concept is possible only if it can be conceptualized as a personally favorable existence.

In an article by Juni and Fischer factors affecting the belief in afterlife were examined. Since the area of death and dying became a rapidly growing area of public and academic interest, the focus in this study was to examine the relationship between religiosity and belief in an afterlife based on data from a national survey. With belief in afterlife as the dependent variable, other factors such as sex, race, age, and marital status were tested. This survey, which included 1,532 respondents, was conducted in 1978 by the National Opinion Research center.

The results indicated that 69.8% (1,069) respondents believe in life after death and 21.2% (325) do not believe. One hundred thirty five respondents (8.8%) selected the "Don't know" response. The breakdown of data by sex showed that 67% of males and 71.8% of females believe in afterlife. The data by race showed that Whites have the highest incidence of belief at 71.5%, while Blacks have a lower incidence of belief at 55.1%. As for age, the 18 to 29 age group had the lowest level of belief (65.4%), the 30 to 59 group had the highest (72%), and the 60+ group had a slightly lower level (70.2%). Married people (71.6%), the divorced (72.4%), and the widowed (71.2%) are among the most likely to believe in life after death. Sixty-six percent of the separated respondents and 60.8% of the singles also expressed belief in an afterlife.

As far as religion was concerned, those claiming no religious preference had low (41.2%) rates of belief in afterlife. Protestants (75.6%) ranked ahead of the Catholic respondents (68.2%). Those of Jewish faith ranked the lowest (17.2%) among all believers in life after death. (This points to the much needed work to be done in this area).

According to church attendance variables, those never attending had the lowest percent of believers in life after death (52.7%). In comparison, those attending in the once-a-week-or-more group had the highest results (83.9%). Religious intensity variables showed that those with a strong (90.7%) or somewhat strong (71.4%) religious intensity are more likely to believe in life after death than those who indicate that their religious intensity is not very strong (66.2%).

Although there has been some indication that religious affiliations have declined recently, Dr. Richard Land, in a BBC News (UK Edition) article dated February 25, 2004, entitled *"How Religion Defined America"* delineates the findings of a January 2004 study indicating that Americans believe in the supernatural (91%), an afterlife (74%), "belief in a God/higher power makes you a better human being" (82%), God or a higher power judged their actions (76%), and perhaps most tellingly "would die for their God/beliefs" (71%).

The positive aspects of religious convictions include the belief that death is a transition to the union with God, that goodness will be rewarded, and that God has chosen one's time of death as part of his beautiful and well-thought-out plan. The negative aspects include that those with increasing death anxiety may believe that they disappointed God, that one will be punished for their sins, and consigned to hell.

Interestingly, Dr. Ian Stevenson, in his book *Children Who Remember Past Lives*, stated: "For most Westerners, life after death has become unthinkable and – along with death itself – a tabooed subject…. Most thinking Westerners would rather not think about…what will happen to me after I die? (Stevenson 317)."

Dr. Gary Schwartz, author of *The Afterlife Experiments*, presents what is billed as breakthrough scientific evidence of life after death. In the book's foreword, Deepak Chopra, a well-known author in the fields of holistic healing and spirituality, writes that Schwartz applies procedures of experimentation regarding questions about the afterlife, and in particular whether we can communicate with the dead, "that no honest skeptic could argue with." Schwartz refers to the theme as the "living soul hypothesis," where he attempts to prove that consciousness survives physical death. The evidence, based on laboratory-controlled results from selected mediums' communications with those who "crossed over," is quite compelling. It lends much credibility to the existence of an afterlife without requiring a leap of faith.

For those who didn't read Schwartz's book, perhaps the greatest fear about dying is thinking that it is a total separation from our loved ones and the end of our existence. For those who take a leap of faith regarding the existence of an afterlife, they are convinced that they will meet their deceased loved ones and God Himself – they claim not to be afraid of death. Yet from another perspective, as shall be specified below, physicians such as Elisabeth Kubler-Ross, Melvin Morse, and Raymond Moody have documented many stories of people who have had near-death experiences. NDEer's souls have journeyed into the afterlife, and then returned to life here. Not only are they not afraid to die, but they also affirm for us that there is a spiritual world beyond.

Chapter Four

The Near Death Experience

*R*esearch has shown that survivors of a near-death experience are almost all changed for the good. They become physically healthier and have fewer psychosomatic complaints. They are happier, exhibit stronger family ties, show more zest for living, and have a greatly diminished fear of death. Similarly, they tend to do more community work, give more charity, and often work in professions that involve helping people. Even those who had a near-death experience as the result of a suicide attempt were found to be significantly less likely to try it again (Morse & Perry 28).

Studies also confirm that virtually everyone who has had an NDE invariably comes to some kind of belief in an afterlife, even those who formerly considered themselves atheists. It follows, then, that the discovery and awareness of one's immortality is the foundation of a healthy psychological constitution. At the very least, it can be said that conviction in one's immortality radically improves the quality of one's present life (Astor 28–29).

In 1975, Raymond Moody Jr. M.D., Ph.D., wrote a highly

popular book entitled *Life After Life*. In it he relayed numerous cases of people who had "died" and been resuscitated. Many had been clinically dead for as long as two minutes, five minutes, even ten minutes and more. These people did not experience a black nothingness, but rather a very rich, vivid set of sensations. They typically go through at least some of the following: They feel their souls separate from and hover over their bodies as they watch everything happening to and around them. They initially feel disoriented as they view their lifeless body and the people who are trying to rescue them. They may also see people who are further away, such as relatives in a waiting room or a nurse getting medication down the hallway, as well as machinery that is being used to revive them that is out of their field of vision. When people try to resuscitate them, their souls don't want to return to their bodies. They are happy and peaceful outside their bodies and have no desire to return to the physical world. Their souls experience utter joy, bliss, and serenity as they travel through a dark tunnel or climb a staircase toward a brilliant light. They enter a world of beauty where the souls of deceased friends, relatives, or religious figures greet them. They feel indescribable pleasure and happiness in this spiritual world where everything is bathed in love and total understanding. Once they meet it, their souls want to be in it forever. Time and space cease to exist, and they know that they are confronting eternity. The Being takes many adults through a life review, showing them everything that they did. Meanwhile, they feel the effects of each of their actions on others (Kaplan). They realize that love and knowledge are two of the most important things that there are. At some point, the Being or the souls that greet the new arrival, explain that it is not yet time for it to stay there. Nevertheless, it is either given a choice to stay forever, or told that it must return to its body. Even though NDEers don't want to return, they go back to their bodies anyway.

From a strict medical viewpoint, they should have seen or felt nothing. Yet, not only could they see and feel, but they experienced sensations that were larger than life, as described above including floating above their bodies and watching the valiant efforts of others to revive them, traveling through a type of tunnel, and encountering deceased relatives or beings of light, or experiencing an all-encompassing warm, restorative light. People who have had these experiences no longer fear death. They know that they have an eternal soul and a task to fulfill on earth before returning to a world of indescribable goodness.

Whereas Kubler-Ross described the process leading up to death, Moody focused on what people experienced as they actually crossed over to the "other side." From the 1960s through the 1980s while Kubler-Ross asked, what happens to us *as* we die? Moody asked, what happens to us *when* we die? In the 1990s the beginnings of attempts were made to look at the afterdeath and their meaning for our lives here. One such researcher is Dr. Sukie Miller, a psychotherapist, whose book, *After Death*, deals with the question of what happens to us *after* we die.

Following Moody, teams of researchers around the world began to study the phenomenon of NDEs in adults. However, even more impressive research collected to date involves cases with children. Most children do not have the motivation to fabricate stories, and those who may have a propensity to stretch the truth couldn't maintain it for the long haul because they would come up short on the details. Therefore, the younger the child undergoing an NDE, the more impressive the case.

In addition to his book *Transformed by the Light*, as noted earlier, Dr. Melvin Morse wrote another well-received book on the subject entitled, *Closer to the Light*, in which he reported the case of Mark, who had an NDE at nine months. At age three, he somehow knew many of the typical core experiences of the NDE. These studies comprise one component of the investigation into the possibility of life after life.

Other scientific attempts into substantiating the existence of survival beyond bodily death actually began over a century ago. Henri Bergson and William James are just two of the more prominent names included in the group that formed the Society for Psychical Research.

The existence of extrasensory perception or ESP demonstrates that we have abilities that are impossible to explain by purely materialistic, mechanistic explanations. If nothing else, it shows that we must be more than our physical bodies. Hence, while skeptics wax eloquent on the questionable existence of ESP, I agree with that segment of the scientific community that finds support for the phenomenon and a rational basis for the belief that something can survive bodily death.

Chapter Five

Out of Body Experiences

Kenneth Ring studied 102 persons using a structured interview schedule that asked a series of probing questions designed to determine the presence or absence of the various components of the core NDE experience as described by Moody. Ring constructed an NDE index, called the Weighted Core Experience Index (WCEI), based on Moody's analysis of the core experience. Scores on the WCEI ranged from zero, indicating an absence of any NDE, to twenty-nine. Sabom found that a score of 6 or higher on the index is evidence of an NDE. The index indicated a core experience incidence rate of 48% in Ring's study. However, the data indicated that core experience incidence may vary as a function of the manner of coming near death, so the core experience incidence rate may differ with different samples. Of Ring's subjects, 95 per cent of those asked stated that the experience was not like a dream (the same result appears in Sabom): they stressed that it was too real, being more vivid and more realistic; however some aspects were hard to express, as the experience did not resemble anything that had happened to them before.

One of Ring's most interesting findings concerned the stages of the experience. He showed that the earlier stages also tended to be reported more frequently. The first stage, peace, was experienced by 60% of his sample, some of whom did not reach any further stages. The next stage was that of 'body separation,' in other words, the OBE (out of body experience). Thirty-seven per cent of Ring's sample reached this stage. Many of Ring's respondents simply described a feeling of being separate or detached from everything that was happening.

Ring tried to find out about two specific aspects of these OBES. First he asked whether they had another body. The answer seemed to be 'no.' Most were unaware of any other body and answered that they were something like 'mind only.'

After the OBE stage comes 'entering the darkness' experienced by nearly a quarter of Ring's subjects. It was described as 'a journey into a black vastness without shape or dimension,' as 'a void, a nothing' and as 'very peaceful blackness.'

For 15% the next stage was reached, 'seeing the light.' The light was sometimes at the end of the tunnel, sometimes glimpsed in the distance but usually it was golden and bright without hurting the eyes. Sometimes the light was associated with a presence of some kind, or a voice telling the person to go back.

Finally there were 10% experiencers who seemed to 'enter the light' and pass into or just glimpse another world. This was described as a world of great beauty, with glorious colors, with meadows of golden grass, birds singing, or beautiful music. It was at this stage that people were greeted by deceased relatives, and it was from this world that they did not want to come back.

Dr. Sabom devoted a chapter in his book *Recollections of Death* to the implications of the near-death experience on the survivor and on the medical community at large. He writes:

"What I have observed convinces me that the NDE is a truly significant event for both the patient and his physician. Moreover, the psychological impact of this experience at the point of near-death may play a role in the physical outcome of the resuscitation itself by affecting a powerful but poorly understood aspect of human life – the "will to live." (Sabom 124)

He goes on to report that death anxiety was dramatically reduced, if not totally eliminated, by the NDEer. Individuals surviving similar types of near-death crisis events without associated NDES, however, did not evidence this change in death fears. Furthermore, this reduction in death anxiety was readily evident not only at the time of the initial interview but also months or years later. Associated with this decrease in death anxiety was the strong personal conviction that the NDE represented a privileged glimpse of what was to occur at the moment of final bodily death. In one case followed by Sabom, a patient said many times before the NDE, "I don't want to die, I'm too young to die;" after it he said, "Well, I'm going to do the best I can, and when my time comes, I'm ready for it" (Sabom 125).

In yet another research study conducted by Dr. Michael Sabom, not only did medically ignorant NDE patients give significantly more accurate accounts of the efforts to save their lives than the control group (cardiac patients who did not have NDES but were asked to describe their ordeals), but the NDE patients could do things like accurately describe the readings on machines not in their "line of sight even if their eyes had been open." This is an amazing phenomenon, and an example of the type of description of a real event that can positively affect someone who believes that death is the absolute end.

In Part One, a number of forms of healing were mentioned, including studies on hypnotherapy and guided imagery. Another form of healing concerns various forms of meditation. One such example, kundalini yoga, is about understanding who we really are, awakening people to their original self, bringing in awareness of the higher self, enlightenment, manifestation and liberation. Another form of healing is through Bibliotherapy.

Chapter Six

Physics and the Metaphysical

*I*n a more tangential connection regarding overcoming the fear of death, there is another whole set of research that Dossey mentions in his book, *Healing Words*, involving a concept that would indeed put people's mind at ease when coping with potentially fatal illness. Physicist Helmut Schmidt of the Mind Science Foundation in San Antonio, Texas, devised some of the earliest and most precise experiments in which subjects tried to influence the output of random event generators (REGs), devices that operate on the basis of truly random radioactive decay or electronic noise, such as occurs in semiconductors. These devices can be made to express their randomness by strings of ones and zeros that are converted into lights or sounds, which the subject tries to influence. This is an indirect way of influencing what nature is doing at the subatomic level.

Other researchers have replicated Schmidts' work independently. Dean Radin and Roger D. Nelson analyzed the results of over 800 studies involving random event generators, conducted between 1959 and 1987. Published in the prestigious journal *Foundations of Physics*, their findings indicated strong evidence for a reliable, replicable direct mental influence on these random natural events. (More recently one of these generators' indicators apparently sensed the September 11, 2001, attacks on the World Trade Center four hours before they happened – but in the fevered mood of conspiracy theories of the time, the claims were swiftly knocked back by skeptics. In December 2004 it also appeared to forewarn of the Asian tsunami just before the deep sea earthquake that precipitated the terrible catastrophe. Today Dr. Nelson is one of the leading researchers in what is referred to as the Global Consciousness Project).

Schmidt then found evidence that these influences may be displaced in time. His subjects tried to influence the output of an REG *in the past* – that is, they tried to affect random events that had already been prerecorded but not yet consciously observed. The outcome: Apparently, present mental 'efforts' were able to influence past events about which 'Nature had not yet made up her mind.'

In what is perhaps an easier context to understand the above, Dossey presented evidence that prayer may indeed influence a past event. For example, consider a person who has recently contracted a terminal cancer. Due to either his or someone else's devoted prayer, he will be spared from dealing with the disease because it will have never actually manifested itself. Somehow the words of the prayer influenced the otherwise pre-determined, inevitable further development and spread of the cancer.

So is death the end of life or is it just a chapter change in the perception of what life is all about? Is there something metaphysical (non-physical) about life? I would like to address these questions via the following published peer-review article.

The *Lancet* article referred to in Part One discussed 344 cardiac patients who were successfully resuscitated after cardiac arrest in ten Dutch hospitals. Demographic, medical, pharmacological, and psychological data were compared between patients who reported an NDE and patients who did not after resuscitation. In a longitudinal study of life changes after an NDE, they compared the groups after 2 and 8 years later.

In their findings, of the 344 patients, sixty-two (18%) reported an NDE. The authors could not figure out why so few cardiac patients reported an NDE. If purely physiological factors resulting from cerebral anoxia caused the NDE, then most of the patients should have had this experience. In the life-change inventory, people who had an NDE had a significant increase in belief in an afterlife ($p = 0.007$) and decrease in fear of death ($p = 0.009$) compared with people who had not had this experience. Depth of NDE was linked to high scores in spiritual items such as interest in the meaning of one's own life, and social items such as showing love and accepting others. All patients, including those who did not have an NDE, had gone through a positive change and were more self-assured, socially aware, and religious than before. Further, people with very deep experiences might be so taken with the experience that they simply allow themselves to slip over to the other side. The sense of what lies ahead of NDEers may be so peaceful, that they simply complete unfinished business here and then let go into death.

The process of change after an NDE took several years to consolidate. One reason for this had to do with society's negative response to NDEers, which lead individuals to deny or suppress their experience for fear of rejection or ridicule. As a result, the effects of the experience can be delayed for years, and only gradually and with difficulty is an NDE accepted and integrated.

The study did not show that psychological, neurophysiological, or physiological factors caused these experiences after cardiac arrest. Sabom mentions a young American woman who had complications during brain surgery for a cerebral aneurysm. The EEG of her cortex and brain stem had become totally flat. After the operation, which was eventually successful, this patient proved to have had a very deep NDE, including an out-of-body experience, with subsequently verified observations during the period of the flat EEG.

The *Lancet* authors continue that neurophysiological processes must nevertheless play some part in an NDE. Similar experiences can be induced through electrical stimulation of the temporal lobe, during neurosurgery for epilepsy, with high carbon dioxide levels and in decreased cerebral perfusion resulting in local cerebral hypoxia as in rapid acceleration during training of fighter-pilots, or as in hyperventilation by valsalva manoeuvre. Ketamine-induced experiences resulting from blockage of the NMDA receptor, and the role of endorphin, serotonin, and enkephalin have also been mentioned, as have near-death-like experiences after the use of LSD, psilocarpine, and mescaline (van Lommel, et al.).

These induced experiences can consist of unconsciousness, out-of-body experiences, and perception of light or flashes of recollection from the past. These recollections, however, consist of fragmented and random memories unlike the panoramic life-review than can occur in an NDE. Further, transformational processes with changing life-insight and disappearance of fear of death are rarely reported after induced experiences. We have already seen through the work of Dossey that deep prayer and meditation can produce events like NDEs, as can other altered states of consciousness, without the person being near death physically.

Getting back to the metaphysical question, the Lancet authors conclude, "the thus far assumed, but never proven, concept that consciousness and memories are localized in the brain should be discussed. How could a clear consciousness outside of one's body be experienced at the moment that the brain no longer functions during a period of clinical death with [a] flat EEG?...NDEs push at the limits of medical ideas about the range of human consciousness and the mind-brain relation" (van Lommel et al.).

Professor Gerald Schroeder, noted physicist and author of three books, *Genesis and the Big Bang: The Discovery of Harmony*

Between Modern Science and the Bible; The Science of God: The Convergence of Scientific and Biblical Wisdom; and *The Hidden Face of God: Science Reveals the Ultimate Truth,* picks up on this theme in a lecture he recently gave in which he delineated a string of proofs claiming that life is metaphysical, and that the scientific community is slowly coming to accept this as a fact. He began by laying out the progression of events emanating from the Big Bang Theory as follows: Big Bang – Energy – Matter – Life – Brain. He then posed the question: is the "mind" in fact part of the brain? According to Professor Schroeder, the mind is *not* shackled to the body. He alluded to Sir James Jeans, an English physicist and mathematician who was the first to propose that matter is continuously created throughout the universe, who said in his book "Mysterious Universe" that the mind is not an accidental intruder into matter. He hails it as the governor of matter. Moreover, for the past fifteen hundred years the Talmud has been teaching that the world is more a thought than a thing. The mind gets in the way of a computer-based chess tournament because the computer is pure calculation – no emotion. Looking at this in a different way, when molecules move through the air to the ear and then to its inner membrane, it mimics the outer membrane via a curved canal, produces a liquid motion whereupon the nerves trigger a signal to the brain. How, then, do we reproduce this sound? After all, there's no sound in the brain. So how do we replay what we hear? The answer appears to be – the mind. The brain is just the radio set and the mind represents the waves that reproduce the sound.

Schroeder then put forth Noble laureate Erwin Schroedinger, author of *My View of the World*, who claims that we do not belong to the physical world – we are actually outsiders, or spectators. We only think we are physical because our bodies are locked in here in this world. *Thought* is what the world is really about.

Schroeder said that in 1954, Professor George Wald, a professor of biology at Harvard, was hired to write an article on the origin of life. He then claimed that time is the hero of the plot – time itself performs the miracles. In 1979, the claim was retracted in an article published in *Scientific American* stating that life could not have started by chance reactions. In the *Journal of Quantum Chemistry*, he expanded upon his work and in 1984 wrote an article called "Life and Mind in the Universe" where he said that he must confess with shock that consciousness and the mind have congruence – that they always existed as a matrix – that they breed life. Schroeder concluded that Professor Wald went from an agnostic to believing that the mind is the basic substance of the universe. In other words, the underlying aspect of the universe is wisdom. "In the beginning" was not really the beginning. In Proverbs 8, God says, "I am wisdom" and in Proverbs 9 God uses wisdom as the basis of existence. Hence, something totally ethereal brings forth the physical. Therefore, there is no problem outliving the physical world.

In the March 2003 edition of *Scientific American*, neurologist professor Robert Sapolsky of Stanford University writes: "We still know squat about how the brain works…we are far from understanding cognitive processes as we were a century ago." Schroeder comments that death is a changing perception of what we are. There is yet a long saga that follows afterwards.

In Genesis Chapter 2:7, the commentary Onkelos tells us that man became a living human. This presumes he was something else before that. In the famous cartoon of the 1950s and 1960s, Casper the Friendly Ghost appeared to his audience as a sheet. That's all we saw. In this world, man is the sheet. There's something else that runs that sheet from underneath.

Dr. Gary Schwartz, the psychologist and researcher referred to earlier regarding his scientific-based work, asked well-known mediums to become part of a series of experiments to prove, or disprove, the existence of an afterlife. He says that it is taken upon faith by modern Western science that mind is a creation of neural structure and function, and that when the brain dies, the mind disappears. However, there is an alternative model, as current as today's visionary science yet as old as recorded history, considered as truth by scholars like Plato and Pythagoras more than two thousand years ago. And it was held by scholars like Sir John Eccles, the Nobel prize-winning neurophysiologist, and Dr. Wilder Penfield, the distinguished neurosurgeon, in the last century. It was also held by Dr. William James, foremost American psychologist and philosopher, Dr. David Bohn, quantum physicist and student of Einstein, and Tom Slick, who established the Mind Science Foundation.

This model says that the mind is first. Consciousness exists independently of the brain; it does not depend upon the brain for its survival. The brain is not the creator of the mind; it is a powerful tool *of* the mind. The brain is like an antenna *for* the mind. Schwartz goes on to describe Columbus's voyage, sailing into the beyond, as a prime example of mediumship experiments in consciousness research. The experiments with mediums suggest that metaphorically, the earth is not flat, it is round. The brain is not primary, the mind is. The mind extends like the light from distant stars. Flat, round; brain, mind – the parallels are eye-opening.

The *Lancet* article alluded to above (van Lommel et al.) allows us to get a glimpse into the non-mechanical causes of death. The authors seem to be saying that there is otherwise no other explanation for why more people didn't have NDEs. In summing up his analysis of this article, Professor Schroeder indicated that for the last 2,000 years Jews have been pre-occupied with sheer survival because of other nations who wished to destroy them. While that still holds true today, Israel's Jews have nevertheless built a strong state from an economic, social and academic point of view. Particularly over the course of the last 30 years, this independence has allowed their collective intellectual capital to focus on such probing issues as: what is there beyond the physical world? Early in his career, John Wheeler, an American theoretical physicist, said that the world is all material. When he reached the age of 90, he said that it's all information (where wisdom, mind and information are all the same – totally ethereal). This is similar to the conclusion of the authors of the *Lancet* article that consciousness may not be localized in the brain.

Dr. Ian Stevenson points out that the evidence for the existence of life after life comes from "not just one type of experience, but from several: apparitions, out-of-body experiences, deathbed visions (i.e. NDES), certain kinds of mediumistic communications, and cases of reincarnation. Of course, when one also adds evidence…gathered from studies on ESP and prayer, the indicators for evidence of survival beyond the grave are even more broadly based" (Stevenson).

George Gallup, Jr. studied American beliefs and conceptions of life after death, through a survey of 1,500 adult Americans. According to Gallup, about one of every seven adult Americans has been close to death at least once, and approximately 5% of the population had an NDE; that is, approximately 35% of individuals who come close to death reported NDES.

Near-death research in the past has focused on the interpretation of NDES. Twemlow, Gabbard, and Jones described 34 NDES and concluded that subjects who had had NDES did not differ from control subjects in terms of psychological health or background. Moreover, they concluded that one does not have to be near death physically in order to have an NDE – just thinking about dying can produce the same effect. Greyson proposed several psychological interpretations of NDES that encompass the paranormal components and beneficial effects of NDES. Lindley, Bryan, and Conley reported a study of 50 NDES and concluded that NDES are not influenced by demographic factors, that NDES produce profound positive personality changes, and that parts of the NDE may be related to endorphins. Carr proposed that certain NDE characteristics are suggestive of a limbic lobe syndrome and may be precipitated in a near-death state by the release of beta-endorphins, giving rise to clinical symptoms such as depersonalization, involuntary memory recall, intense emotions, and hallucinations.

"Permission to believe is not based merely on wishful thinking or tradition; neither is it permission extended only to those who have had firsthand experience. Rather, it is permission granted to all on the basis of the evidence – evidence collected by some hard-nosed scientists who measure their words very, very carefully. Therefore, if you need permission from the scientific, rationally-based worldview to believe in survival beyond bodily death, know that such permission has been granted" (Astor 41–42).

Parapsychology is another field in which the issue of immortality has been studied. Parapsychology is the scientific study of paranormal phenomena – unusual experiences that do not seem to be explainable in terms of our everyday understanding or known scientific principles. Typically this involves spontaneous contact with the dead or dying. There are a vast amount of reports and accounts of individuals of all ages who have had some contact with the already deceased dating back to the 1800s. These unusual occurences represent another set of cases in the study of life after death. Widows commonly report having contact with their deceased spouses. In their book *Death and Ethnicity*, Kalish and Reynolds state that over 50% of the women and over 30% of the men they studied reported some sort of contact with the dead. These experiences were extremely meaningful to these people because it changed their feelings about death.

Chapter Seven

Logotherapy /
Existentialist Theory

*I*n *Man's Search for Meaning*, Dr. Viktor Frankl, an accomplished Viennese psychiatrist and philosopher, wrote, "Life in a concentration camp tore open the human soul and exposed its depths…The experiences of camp life show that man does have a choice of action…. There were always choices to make. Every day, every hour, offered the opportunity to make a decision, a decision which determined whether you would or would not submit to those powers which threatened to rob you of your very self, your inner freedom…"

This was his way of overcoming his fear of death. Life, even in the horror of a concentration camp, was not meaningless. He trained himself to go to a state of mind whenever he chose to. That was his personal freedom – no one could take that away from him. When he realized it, it gave him the hope that ultimately made him a survivor of those Nazi camps. Later on through his writings, his contribution to society gave hope to many others who doubted their self worth and sense of purpose. He survived because he took control of his thoughts. "Everyone," he wrote, "has his own specific vocation or mission in life to carry out a concrete assignment which demands fulfillment. Therein he cannot be replaced, nor can his life be repeated. Thus, everyone's task is as unique as is his specific opportunity to implement it" (Frankl 113).

From an evolutionary point of view, organisms must deal with a number of universal existential issues if they are to survive and reproduce. One is the issue of hierarchy, that is, where one fits in the vertical dimension of social life. A second issue is concerned with territoriality, that is, learning what parts of the environment and of the body belong to the core of the self. Clinical problems associated with boundary issues and control issues are related to territorial conflicts. The third universal existential issue is concerned with identity, which from a clinically oriented view deals with the question of who we are. Crises of identity are common in therapeutic practice particularly among adolescents and those going through a midlife crisis. The fourth issue, temporality, is related to the universality of death and with the need to cope with the anxieties connected with it (Plutchik).

Logotherapy is a meaning-oriented approach to therapy, among the humanistic and existentialist schools of thought. It has applications in many areas of the Health-sciences and Humanities. At the core of Logotherapy is the belief that the search for ultimate meaning in life is a fundamental human motivating force. It recognizes that having a sense of meaning in life is essential for our well being. Even in facing death and suffering, by showing courage we can turn a situation into a supremely meaningful one.

Frankl's experiences validated his former conceptualization of the basic principles of Logotherapy, according to which everything can be taken away from us, except the freedom in our spirit to choose the attitude we take toward the circumstances in our life. As far as a therapeutic modality, Logotherapy can be used in helping people cope with phobias by Paradoxical Intention. In other words, Logotherapy can be seen as "dereflecting" the patient away from their presenting problem towards searching for meaning. The patient is dereflected from their disturbance to something other than themselves.

In an evaluation tool called the Spirituality Change Survey, Kubler-Ross quotes John Alexander (who developed this as part of his doctoral dissertation at Walden University) in his comparing pre and post-workshop attitudes of participants on death:

PRE: "end, termination, sorrow, emptiness"
POST: "peaceful, absence of fear"
PRE: "fear, the end, terrifying, pain"
POST: "moving on, it's OK"
PRE: "an escape from life"
POST: part of a continuum, a transition"

There have been a number of studies showing that not all NDES are positive. In his book *Beyond Death's Door*, Dr. Maurice Rawlings, a Tennessee cardiologist, reported that 20% of his patients who were resuscitated after a heart attack had an unpleasant out-of-body experience, such as finding themselves in hell (Rawlings). He added that most tended to forget this experience. He further claimed that his results were more valid than those of other researchers who report overwhelmingly positive experiences by their patients. The reason he believes his research is more accurate is due to the fact that he interviewed his patients almost immediately after the event, as opposed to others who only conducted such interviews weeks or months later.

Another study conducted by Dr. Charles Garfield, a psychologist at The University of California at San Francisco Cancer Research Institute, showed that approximately 11% of his NDE patients saw images of demons and had nightmares. While the majority still reported positive experiences, it is important to be aware that not all NDES ended up being spiritually or otherwise uplifted.

Chapter Eight

Treating Phobias

*T*he successful treatment of traditionally physical ailments with past-life regressions puts those illnesses into the realm of a mentally treatable disease, similar to that of a phobia (Moody & Perry). Phobias are an exaggerated and usually inexplicable and illogical fear of a particular object or class of objects, such as darkness, flying in an airplane, elevators, being buried alive, animals, and bridges. Between 10% and 20% of the population will develop phobias during their lives. Past-life regressions have been successful in treating phobias because they serve to bring these fears to the fore, explaining them on a conscious level.

Moody quotes a study conducted by Johannes M. Cladder of The Netherlands that dealt with the treatment of difficult phobics (patients who had previous psychotherapy and in some cases hospitalization), in which 20 out of 25 patients got rid of their phobias through past-life regression therapy. It took the patients who had been previously hospitalized an average of fifteen sessions to improve, while the patients who had not been hospitalized showed significant improvement after ten sessions. Cladder concluded that past-life therapy is a quick and effective means of dealing with phobias.

There are a number of standard approaches used by therapists to modify the actions and thought patterns of people suffering from phobias. Unfortunately, about three quarters of people with phobias never get help. Many people with phobias are reluctant to seek assistance because of embarrassment. Others don't understand what they have or where to find help, while still others fear the treatment itself.

A key component of most treatments is behavior therapy, designed to alter the way a person acts. Behavior therapy typically involves gradual exposure of the patient to the feared situation.

Behavior techniques are often combined with cognitive therapy that aims to change the way that people view themselves and their fears. Rather than thinking, "I am frightened and might have a panic attack," the individual is encouraged to assess the situation in a more positive way, perhaps thinking, "I am frightened, but I am not in danger." The patient is trained to analyze his feelings and separate realistic from unrealistic situations.

Exposure therapy, which is part of behavior therapy, works by gradually exposing the individual to the feared object or situation. Facing the feared situation helps the patient see that he can cope successfully, and that escape is unnecessary. Over time, the individual gains greater control over the anxiety so that ultimately he can face the threatening situation or object with little or no fear.

There are a number of variations to exposure therapy. The degree of exposure will vary depending on the therapist's assessment of the patient. The feared situation, such as giving a speech, may be simulated, or the person with the disorder may be placed in a real situation that he fears, such as driving over a bridge. Treatment of a phobia can be conducted individually or in a group.

In his chapter on "Dealing with the Fear of Death," Burns does not consider dealing with the fear of death an issue that is particularly difficult to overcome. In the chapter dealing with this phobia, he breaks down the essence of the fear into three stages: the dying process (up to the point when one passes into unconsciousness), the actual moment of death (the instant one slips into consciousness), and after one has died.

Burns claims that the first stage is actually a fear of life, not of death. If one has been able in the past to overcome an illness, discomfort, and even pain, then he sees no reason why one cannot cope again. How was it handled before? If via medication, then that option is available again. Someone in great agony from a terminal illness is usually not afraid of death – they actually welcome the opportunity to be taken out of their misery. He goes on to say that for those who are "afraid" of not having accomplished what they would have liked to, these people are actually perfectionists, and are not really afraid of death.

The second stage is likened to going to sleep. If one has no fear of falling asleep and waking up the next morning, then why be afraid of the moment of dying? "One moment you're conscious, and at the next instant you're asleep. There's literally nothing to it."

The third stage is even easier. When you sleep you are not aware of your surroundings; likewise in death. He reframes negative thoughts and by a process of cognitive behavior therapy rationalizes away these negative thoughts. Burns then proposes thinking more positively by having a person imagine how uncomfortable it would be if everybody in this world stopped growing old at age twenty-one and lived forever. Someone with claustrophobia would go insane because there would be no room to escape. Likewise, if someone was smashed to bits in a car crash and couldn't die – Burns asks: "Now are you so sure that death is such a bad thing?" He ends his chapter by quoting his then eight-year old son who said, "people wouldn't worry so much about death if they were having fun."

Some of Burns' techniques seem simple enough to implement and sound rational. A therapist would do well to be equipped with some of these techniques as they may help some people. I am not as yet convinced that these rationalizations are enough to overcome this fear completely, especially for those who are not cognitive (rational, thinking) people. A combination of emotional and factual information about the journey of a soul, the meaning of life, reincarnation, and the afterworld may go a longer way in dissolving this fear and subsequently maintaining a healthy and positive outlook.

Chapter Nine

Encounters with Death
in Motion Pictures

The entertainment industry, known for producing a wide selection of shows for viewing on television, screening in the movies, or performing on stage, has taken on a number of challenging projects involving the near-death experience. Two such movies, *Flatliners* and *Fearless*, present a vivid yet suspenseful look at individuals who died and came back to tell about it. Despite the fact that both movies focused more on the short-term negative effects of the NDE than on the positive, the overall message to learn from these experiences en route to becoming a better person came through.

Flatliners (1990), a film directed by Joel Schumacher, is a story of a small group of medical students experiencing clinical death who actually outbid each other for length of time being dead. After a few minutes of induced death, they "come back" to life and begin to be haunted by their sins and misdeeds, which harm them both physically and mentally. In the *Lancet* article reviewed above we noted that the various methods available to induce death have not proven to yield the same kinds of experiences as real NDEers had. In this movie, since the medical students induced each other's temporary death, what they saw while clinically dead was not equivalent to what has been reported by individuals who went through a real NDE. Nevertheless, we get the sense that there is "something" out there beyond this world.

Professor John Wren-Lewis wrote a review of Peter Weir's film *Fearless* (1993), which first appeared in *Pallicom*, a hospice journal in Australia. The film's protagonist has flashbacks to events that occurred when his flight home from Texas to San Francisco crashed somewhere in prairie country. The movie portrays the fundamental feeling of a near-death experience, and why lives are subsequently changed.

It is still not at all widely realized that all the classical experiences which make the headlines when people are resuscitated from the brink of clinical death – disappearance of fear and pain, feelings of blissful peace, slowing down or total stoppage of time, even the famous tunnel and encounter with celestial beings and heavenly light – can also occur to people who like the movie's protagonist, narrowly avoid death without being sick or damaged in any way.

One of the very first serious studies in this field was made by a Swiss alpine climber named Albert Heim back in the 1890s, who fell off a cliff to what seemed like certain death, only to land on soft snow with very minor injuries. As he went down, time seemed to become infinitely extended, fear vanished, as he experienced wonderful colors and music, plus a panoramic review of his life right from childhood. He was moved to write a scientific paper about it when he found many other mountaineers had similar experiences, but this received little if any attention outside Switzerland, and wasn't translated into English until Professor Russell Noyes of the University of Iowa did so in the 1970s, after Raymond Moody had begun to draw attention through his research and publications (Lewis).

Even then very little attention was paid to *this* kind of NDE because journalists – and, for that matter, most professional researchers – were concerned mainly with finding possible evidence of a soul that could survive the body's death, which meant concentrating on people who actually have been dead for a short period (as in *Flatliners*). The movie shows how the protagonist's calm rescue of other passengers was indeed no heroic defiance but something he can do quite naturally because time has slowed down for him, enabling him to see how to avoid falling debris, and so on.

Why is it, continues Lewis, that something like a close brush with death is normally needed for the heavenliness of the world to be experienced? The film's answer seems to be that the natural biological fear-response seems to have gotten out of hand in the human species, to the point where it governs the whole organization of social life sown to the minutest detail, blocking out aliveness in the process. Coming close to death unravels the knot, but then we have the problem of finding out how to organize such practical affairs with fear as life's servant rather than its master, something about which even the world's greatest experts and religious teachers have left us with only very partial blueprints.

In another movie entitled *Angels in the Endzone* (1997), a high school football player who lost his father in a car accident scores the winning touchdown for his team, and as he crosses the goal line, time stops and he is visited by his deceased father. The son looks at the angelic figure that appears exactly as he knew him when he was alive, and asks: "Why did you leave me, Dad?" To which his father replies: "I never did; I never will, son." This very powerful ending to this movie gave the son an understanding that he didn't appreciate for many months after his father passed on. He came to realize that a loved one who departs from this world is still very much alive and is watching from above. The movie's writers made a point of ensuring that this positive note be emphasized.

In what was personally my favorite film on the subject filled with a very positive, feel-good image of the World to Come, *Field of Dreams* (1989) captures the world of fantasy in a way that makes it very believable. Earlier I discussed the notion of the metaphysical regarding the workings of our mind. Well, we have here a formula that for some sums up life in this world:

Baseball + Metaphysics = Perfection

Director Phil Alden Robinson's *Field of Dreams* pays homage to baseball's majestic, magical link to nostalgia. When a struggling Iowa farmer, Ray Kinsella (Kevin Costner) begins "hearing voices" and subsequently plows under his cornfield and builds a baseball diamond, he becomes a pariah to his community and to his family. But Ray knows he's tapped into a special level of consciousness: a beautiful, soothing karma that slowly but wonderfully manifests itself throughout this incredible film. The baseball field itself becomes a portal to another world, enabling players from baseball's Golden Age to return.

During the course of the movie the audience is aware that beyond a certain point on the field it is forbidden for mortals to set foot. The deceased players, who come back each day to play on the field, enter from a specific plane in the distant outfield. Beyond that point is a mystery to humans. It represents the crossover to the next world. However, it makes one realize how easy it is to make the crossover back and forth. When one of the film's protagonists very desperately wants to go beyond the line to see what is there, he is warned that once he crosses over, he may not come back. In a stirring display of courage and faith, he takes a slow step toward the other side, pokes his head through as if looking beyond a curtain, and begins to laugh like a little child who sees a store full of candy and ice cream that is his for the taking. He then proceeds with full confidence to the other side.

The important message that he left behind for the other movie characters and for the movie's audience was, "Hey, dying is nothing to be afraid of. It is just a gateway to another dimension – one in which there is full life, perhaps even a better one than the one we are in at the moment."

Chapter Ten

Virtual Reality as a Treatment Modality

*T*he use of virtual reality in dealing with phobias is in its infancy. We are beginning to see more papers being published since the first few appeared in journals during the course of the last seven to eight years. As mentioned earlier in this section, the two most common phobias that virtual reality has begun to address are fear of flying and fear of public speaking. The technology is still a bit awkward and hence, while early testing points to positive results in affecting a decrease in a person's phobia, there is still much work to be done to perfect aspects of the technology such as the less than realistic images that appear in the helmet, to the heaviness of the helmet itself, to the exorbitant cost of purchasing a system for use in a clinical setting.

Researchers at Haifa University, working with colleagues at the University of Washington in Seattle, have developed a virtual reality program to help victims of suicide bombings cope with their experiences (*Jewish Tribune*, July 1, 2004). The universities have created multi-disciplinary teams to treat victims and have found that, through six one-hour therapy sessions, they make progress in treating their patients' post-traumatic stress disorder (PTSD). While the Israeli university is assisting victims of suicide bombings, the American institution is applying the treatment program to people affected by the terrorist attacks on the World Trade Center in New York.

The treatment program sees patients gradually and systematically exposed to their terrifying experience. During the virtual reality exposure therapy, patients wear a virtual-reality helmet that positions two goggle-sized miniature computer monitor screens close to the patient's eyes. Patients have the illusion that they are really on the Haifa street where a suicide bus bombing took place.

A random sampling of publications on the use of virtual reality in treatment shows that the majority deal with human-computer interaction, followed by uses in psychotherapy, fear of flying, in post-traumatic stress disorder (PTSD), anxiety, exposure therapy and acrophobia.

The National Institute on Drug Abuse (NIDA), at the National Institutes of Health, sponsored a one-day symposium entitled "Virtual Reality: Opportunities for the National Institutes of Health" on February 24, 2004, featuring leading experts who are using virtual reality (VR) in healthcare. Specific topic areas included treatment and evaluation of anxiety disorders, post-traumatic stress disorder (PTSD), obesity and eating disorders, cue exposure for drug treatment, distraction during painful medical procedures, and explorations for using VR in neuro-rehabilitation and physical therapy. The conference then concluded with a discussion of potential new uses for VR, current technical issues and limitations, and potential new targets for funding by the institutes.

This NIH conference followed the 3-day Cyber Therapy 2004 Conference (www.vrphobia.com) held January 10–12 in San Diego, CA. The conference, organized by the Interactive Media Institute (IMI), began with a 1-day series of workshops covering basic aspects of clinical VR applications and an introductory workshop that focused on currently available equipment and technical issues. Over 100 speakers from 15 countries presented controlled clinical trials on using VR for mental health care treatment and training healthcare providers, and showcased many cutting-edge applications including VR for schizophrenia, autism, HIV counseling, and prevention. Fear of death was not a featured treatment option.

Some therapists use virtual reality to desensitize patients to the thing they fear. Other forms of therapy that may be of benefit to phobics are graduated exposure therapy and cognitive behavioral theory (CBT). Anti-anxiety medication can also be of assistance in some cases. Most phobics understand that they are suffering from an irrational fear, but are powerless to override their initial panic reaction.

Graduated Exposure and CBT both work towards the goal of desensitizing the sufferer, and changing the thought patterns that are contributing to their panic. Gradual desensitization treatment and CBT are often extremely successful, provided the phobic is willing to make a continuous effort over a long period of time. Practitioners of neuro-linguistic programming (NLP) claim to have a procedure that can be used to alleviate most specific phobias in a single therapeutic session, however, this has not yet been verified scientifically.

Virtual reality (VR) technology is administered by a psychotherapist who operates the computer software while providing counseling. Each virtual reality session lasts about an hour, and runs anywhere from 8 to 10 sessions. The technology works this way: The patient is seated comfortably next to a computer. They'll put on a headset that provides 3-D animation and sound, and experience what they're afraid of. For example, if you're afraid of flying, you'll see animation of what it's like to be in the passenger seat. You'll also be able to look out a window and see the plane moving on the runway, taking off, flying and landing.

One of the leaders in virtual reality treatment is Dr. Joanne Difede, a psychologist at Weill Cornell Medical College's Department of Psychiatry in New York. Difede has been using virtual reality exposure therapy on her patients who suffer from anxiety and post-traumatic stress disorder (PTSD) due to 9/11, and other simple phobias like fear of flying, heights and closed spaces. She set up the first clinical program in the Northeast to use virtual reality exposure therapy to treat post-traumatic stress disorder and, it is one of the few VR treatment facilities in the nation.

The PTSD system, which depicts the World Trade Center on September 11, was co-developed by Dr. Difede and Dr. Hunter Hoffman, a researcher at the University of Washington. Dr. Difede believes that patients must confront what they fear in order to improve and become desensitized to it. This is actually how imaginal exposure therapy, the standard treatment for PTSD and phobias, has worked as well. A therapist encourages patients to imagine what frightens them and to talk about it. But, for many patients, especially those with PTSD or phobias, this can be a problem because inherent in the ailments is the tendency to avoid fear, and this leaves many patients unwilling or unable to "open up." This is where virtual reality has a real advantage.

By putting on a VR helmet, the patient is immediately immersed into a three-dimensional environment. When they look down or sideways, the scenery shifts. According to Dr. Difede, it encourages the patient to emotionally engage. Virtual reality offers the therapist and patient total control over their environment and the ability to proceed at an individualized pace. In treating phobias such as fear of flying, a smooth flight might precede one with dark skies and turbulence.

Dr. Difede also collaborated with Dr. Barbara Rothbaum of Emory University to introduce the use of Seromycin into their virtual reality therapy sessions. Seromycin, a medication that is currently used to treat tuberculosis, but it has also been found to aid in the transmission of a key protein to a certain brain receptor. The medication can speed a patient's "unlearning" of a particular fear and reduce the number of VR sessions needed to perhaps two. Typically, most patients now require about six or seven one-hour sessions.

We see from the above that fear of death was not ranked high in their order of phobia priorities. Nonetheless, technological advancement in virtual reality should be watched closely and considered as a potentially viable treatment modality for those who fear death.

Chapter Eleven

Mortality Salience /
Terror Management

We now move from virtual reality to cite a number of studies on mortality salience and terror management. There are certain groups of people who are labeled as *stigmatized*. Examples of such "out-groups" are persons with physical disabilities, mental illness, and welfare recipients. Stigmatized groups are viewed negatively, but the underlying causes are not all that clear. Two areas have been examined that may aid in understanding why this phenomenon occurs (Guthrie). The mortality salience hypothesis states that people will be more likely to hold negative attitudes toward out-groups when an awareness of inevitable death does not support their existing beliefs (Pyszczynski, Greenberg, & Solomon). Secondly, framing has been examined and has been defined as the context in which information is portrayed (Iyengar; Nelson & Oxley). Does the medium used to convey information have a greater effect on people's attitudes toward out-groups or does the realization that life will one day end in death create a greater impact on our attitudes?

Becker pointed out that people realize at a relatively young age that death is inevitable. It is embedded into young minds that we will eventually die. Instead of observing this fact, people ignore it by possessing certain beliefs, such as organized religion, in order to protect them from the threat death educes. This point can be further argued to claim that all human behavior is designed to protect us from dying.

It is interesting to note that we all have the capability to take ourselves in and out of certain states during the course of a regular day. When one gets stuck, one may seek the help of a therapist to get out of the rut. Short of exposing the patient to the harsh realities of a past emotional event, there are techniques that assist the patient to deal with the problem. Distancing, speed, changing the perspective of the event (thereby changing the emotional reaction to that same event), seeing an event as an outsider, from a point above, seeking out how the patient felt in the past before the event or asking the patient to project what he would look like in the future after the event, equipping the individual with tools that he could imagine taking back to the scene of the disturbing event – all of the above (Paltiel) are tools used in order not to get the same kinesthetic. For example, phobias are referred to as *synethesias* – that is, the simultaneous overlapping of two representational systems, or when two systems become "glued" together. This is expressed as:

$$Vr + Ar = V/K$$

The aim is to separate between the visual (V) image of the event and the kinesthetic (K) feeling and try to look at them differently.

Manipulation enters less into the picture if the patient comes in to the therapist's session with enthusiasm and motivation toward fixing the problem because they'll have a natural incentive to wanting to overcome their issue.

The first ethical responsibility of therapists, regardless of what values they espouse, is to be fully aware of what they communicate to their clients. Equally important is to be respectful towards the clients' values and not to impose their own on them. Psychotherapists are sometimes criticized for psycho-engineering – that is, manipulating clients not for their own welfare but for what is thought to be a good role adjustment. Family therapists are usually singled out in particular for such manipulation. Behavioral and dynamic family therapists disagree about the way therapies should be carried out; both systems are characterized by "school" values as well as the values of the particular therapist. As behaviorists O'Leary and Turkewitz acknowledge, "While we strive not to have our values unduly influence our clients, it seems clear that we do influence them by the questions we ask…and by the therapeutic targets we help establish…. This can lead to a bias left unsaid which may result in a more subtle or insidious influence process which can be counterproductive" (Lakin 22).

In her review of Martin Lakin's book, *Ethical Issues in the Psychotherapies*, Emma Pavato writes that Lakin explores such issues as the therapist as parent substitute or moral guide. The prescriptive vs. Socratic approaches to the identification of a clear set of values for the client to use as a frame of reference is discussed in terms of individual differences in client's strengths and needs and resultant legitimate variations in effective intervention strategies. Although there is a widespread agreement that psychotherapists should strive to keep their own values to themselves Lakin points out that: "Frequently the emotional state of the person seems to demand directive actions by the therapist that contradict the principal of personal autonomy and self-choosing."

While boasting individual freedom, human behavior and thinking is sometimes controlled subtly by advertisers, political candidates, government officials, military leaders, counselors, employers, preachers, news media, social norms, and economic developments in the society. Publishing houses and research funding organizations manipulate writers and researchers in their work. Parents manipulate their children, and children soon become skilled in manipulating adults. Teachers and students are involved in similar mutual manipulation. Even husbands and wives attempt, at times, to control each other's behavior.

But the scientific investigation of behavior manipulation has not been limited to psychology. Biologists, geneticists, pharmacologists, economists, physiologists, sociologists, communication experts, and others have studied the problem empirically and have shown that human behavior can be altered and controlled with a high degree of efficiency. Some examples include shock or other physical stimulation, surgery and electrical stimulation of the brain, manipulation of genes, drugs, group pressure, mass media, hypnosis, persuasion, education, or the arousal of fear.

In an article written by Gary Collins, "The Manipulation of Human Behavior," the author says that control or manipulation can be defined as the changing of environmental conditions to which an organism is exposed so as to bring about a definite behavioral result. The result may be a production of new behavior, maintenance of existing behavior, and/or an elimination of undesirable behavior.

He further states that by administering desirable reinforcement following acceptable behavior, and withholding reinforcement following undesirable behavior psychologists have been able to change the behavior of uncooperative children so that they cooperate; modify the behavior of mute psychotic patients so that they talk; control the actions of schizophrenics; eliminate thumb-sucking, stealing, crying, tantrums, stuttering, excessive vomiting, hyperactivity, and social withdrawal in children; control overeating; eliminate phobias; train retarded children; treat neurotics; and eliminate undesirable sex behavior. Dr. B.F. Skinner (1968), the man who started most of this, has himself shown how teaching machines can provide reinforcement at the most desirable time and bring about more efficient learning.

Psychotherapy has been defined as:

A form of treatment for problems of an emotional nature in which a trained person deliberately establishes a professional relationship with a patient with the object of removing, modifying or retarding existing symptoms, of mediating disturbed patterns of behavior, and of promoting positive personality growth and development. (Wolberg)

For Collins, this is another way of saying that psychotherapy is a procedure wherein a professionally trained person, known as a therapist, seeks to manipulate, control, and modify the behavior of another person, known variously as a patient, client, or counselee.

Of course psychotherapy is not exclusively a function of psychologists. Psychiatrists, social workers, pastoral counselors, and many others spend their lives attempting to help distraught, confused and unhappy people to change their behavior in ways that will make their lives happier.

Psychotherapists use different techniques and have different goals, depending somewhat on the patient's problem and on the therapist's personality, abilities, and theoretical position. Some therapists attempt to change behavior by encouragement, support, and reassurance; some try to promote patient insight into problems; some try to teach new methods of behavior; some encourage patient expression and ventilation of pent-up feelings; some give advice and suggestions; some make interpretive statements about patient behavior; some work with individuals; some work with groups. Most therapists use a combination of these techniques.

Undoubtedly psychotherapists do control and modify behavior to varying extents. However, we are less likely to manipulate others when we remember that each of us has feelings, aspirations, frustrations, and hopes.

Having stated the moral obligations of utilizing the art of manipulation, our attitudes toward people depend on the groups to which they belong (Pyszczynski, Greenberg, & Solomon). The awareness of death manifests itself as anxiety, which is maintained by a belief system or the worldview, and consequently guides societal living. The problem arises when people do not conform to our worldviews.

Beliefs toward out-groups are ultimately affected by an awareness of death because they are either supported or not supported by different groups' worldviews. When people were aware of their death, they perceived people who belonged to the same religious group positively, while viewing religious out-groups negatively.

Further, when they were aware of their death, people mandated that out-groupers receive harsher sentences for being "moral transgressors." In a second study, Rosenblatt et al. claimed that it was because of the particular moral beliefs that people upheld that they perceived out-groups negatively. Conflicting beliefs elicit negative reactions toward dissimilar others because they do not affirm people's worldviews.

When beliefs were affirmed, out-groups were not necessarily viewed negatively, but were perceived according to people's existing beliefs. This supports the idea that there is a tendency for people to uphold their beliefs in the face of death. Additionally, if people's attitudes are found to be negative, it can be inferred that those attitudes were negative initially, and merely strengthened after people were induced with an awareness of death.

Greenberg et al. found that when people realized they were going to die and had been given information about tolerance, their attitudes were less negative than when tolerance was not primed. This follows that attitudes toward out-groups are dependent upon the type of information that someone receives. In other words, even though only some people were unconsciously aware of the effects of priming, tolerance stimuli did not affect everyone's attitudes. It can be concluded, then, when particulars are provided, attitudes change, regardless of whether people consciously register that information.

Analyses indicated that people aware of their death were more likely to exhibit in-group favoritism. Simply reading something that elicits an awareness of death alters our attitudes in a negative manner toward out-groups. This runs consistent to past findings that have also suggested death awareness negatively alters people's perceptions of dissimilar others.

The terror management theory, pioneered by Harvard psychologist Ernest Becker, contends that people adopt beliefs about reality to shield themselves from two unacceptable truths: The world is dangerous, and the only certainty is death. Cultures evolved to manage that terror, and they react violently when threatened by an outside person, group, or idea. In other words, a set of personal or cultural practices or beliefs enables an individual or a society to ignore or accept the inevitability of death. Terror management theory assumes that humans spend a great deal of psychological energy in their attempts to manage or deny their subconscious terror. It may lead to cognitive construction of immortality through attaching oneself psychologically to institutions, traditions, or symbols. When these constructs are threatened, one would resort to anger and violence to bolster their sense of security and protect their illusion of immortality.

Terror management theory proposes that reminders of our mortality (which result in mortality salience [MS]) produce strong anxiety that people are motivated to reduce. One typical MS manipulation is for patients to write essays about what they think will happen to them as they die, and about their thoughts and feelings about death.

Research supporting terror management theory has shown that participants facing their death (via MS) exhibit more greed than do control participants. In a recent study (Cozzolino, Staples, Meyers, & Samboceti), the authors look to reports of near-death experiences and post-traumatic growth which reveal that many people who nearly die come to view seeking wealth and possessions as empty and meaningless. Guided by these reports, a manipulation called death reflection was generated. Highly extrinsic participants who experienced death reflection exhibited intrinsic behavior. Death reflection and mortality salience manipulations were then compared. Results showed that mortality salience led highly extrinsic participants to manifest greed, whereas death reflection again generated intrinsic, unselfish behavior.

Furthermore, terror management theory hinges on the premise that people are aware of and troubled by their own mortality (Pyszczynski et al.). In other words, people realize that they are going to die and this knowledge creates fear. The resulting anxieties are seen as triggering a wide variety of behaviors that overtly or covertly mitigate the threat of death. In addition, these fears and the responses to them often act as a catalyst for a wide range of dysfunctional behaviors or hostile responses. (Interestingly, by contrast, Kubler-Ross reports in her experience with children in her book *On Children and Death* that they often come to terms with their mortality and communicate this via their drawing of flowers, birds, balloons and butterflies as predictors of when they will die). However, leading scholars in terror management theory, Solomon, Greenberg, and Pyszczynski argue that human consciousness gives rise to patterns of denying vulnerability, helplessness, insignificance, and mortality. This shared cultural construction enables people to lead relatively anxiety-free lives and regain a sense of immortality to the extent that they can perceive themselves to be living up to cultural standards.

Michael Salzman, a terror management theorist, points out that when people can identify with a cultural/social heritage they are better able to cope with their mortality since their traditions provide a feeling of belonging to something that is more permanent than they are. The terror management model employs two interlocking theories: the anxiety-buffer hypothesis and the mortality-salience hypothesis.

The anxiety-buffer hypothesis "states that if a psychological structure provides protection against anxiety, then augmenting that structure should reduce anxiety" (Salzman 175). On the other hand "the mortality-salience hypothesis states that if a psychological structure provides protection against the terror inherent in human existence (knowledge of mortality), then reminding people of their mortality should increase their need for the protection provided by the structure" (175).

Walle, building upon terror management theory and Salzman's use of it, provides a more in-depth analysis of cultural disruption and how it triggers dysfunctional behavior. According to Walle, significant contact with the powerful outside world can lead to social stress and cultural decline, that is to say, challenges to the belief systems of the culture. That, in turn, gives rise to hurtful and counterproductive responses. In his analysis, Walle argues that people typically use their culture as a buffer against anxiety. When the culture is weakened by threat or a strong challenge, however, it is less able to serve in this role and, as a result, anxiety and the dysfunctional behavior triggered by it tend to increase.

The key to this model is the assumption that under normal circumstances people are comforted by their culture and society because these social constructs transcend them and these overarching cultural phenomena typically survive the death of the individual. Thus, by identifying with an ongoing heritage and legacy, people are often able to relieve their anxieties by gaining a sense of collective immortality.

Afterword

s far as bibliotherapy is concerned, there is evidence that suggests that reading can affect positive change in people. Having an NDEer tell his/her story live can be at least as powerful as bibliotherapy because it is real. Hypnotherapy has been used for many years for many different purposes with success in alleviating issues buried in the past. Movies also have a strong affect on people's attitudes. These four methods have not been documented in the literature as having been used in specific reference to therapeutic interventions for fear of death therapy. Furthermore, these interventions are not novel by any stretch of the imagination, however, if used selectively for the direct purpose of alleviating one's fear of death, then perhaps, together, they can affect more of a change than any single modality can achieve by itself. One therapist I know told me that it matters less which one worked best – what matters is whether the patient was helped by any combination of these methods.

Glossary

bet midrash: study hall

chavruta (pl. *chavrutot*): learning partner

HaCohen: the priest

Haftara: reading from the books of the Prophets that follows the Torah reading on Sabbaths and holidays

Hamelech: "the king"

Hashem: literally, "the [Divine] Name," God

hesped: eulogy

midrash: Jewish commentaries on the Hebrew scriptures compiled between 400 and 1200 CE and based on exegesis, parable and legend

Moshe Rabbeinu: lit. "Moses our Teacher," Moses

Naaseh v'nishma: "We will do and we will listen." This is what the Jewish people said to God upon receiving the Torah.

olam haba: the World to Come

Parasha: Torah portion of the week

rabbanim: rabbis

Shir Hashirim: the Song of Songs

shul: synagogue

Sifri: commentary on the books of Numbers and Deuteronomy

tikkun: repairing

Yaakov Avinu: The Patriarch Jacob

Yitzchok Avinu: the Patriarch Isaac

References

Achterberg, J., & Lawlis, G. Frank. (1984). *Imagery and Disease.* Champaign, IL: After Death Communication Research Foundation. *http://www.adcrf.org*

Aiken, L. (1996). *Why Me, God?* New Jersey: Jason Aronson Inc.

Ajzen, I. (2001). Nature and operation of attitudes. *Annual Review of Psychology, 52.*

Alvarado, K.A., Templer, D.I., Bresler, C., & Thomas-Dobson, S. (1995). The relationship of religious variables to death depression and death anxiety. *Journal of Clinical Psychology,* 51, 202–204.

Astor, Y. (2003). *Soul Searching.* Southfield, Michigan: Targum Press.

Atwater, P.M.H. (1988). *Coming Back to Life: The After-effects of the Near-Death Experience.* New York: Dodd, Mead and Company.

Becker, E. (1973). *The Denial of Death.* New York: The Free Press.

Bede, The Venerable (1968). *A History of the English Church and People.* England: Penguin Books.

Bell, L. (2000). *Happy Endings.* Florida: Quality of Life Publishing.

ben Horcanos HaGadol, E., Rabbi (c. 100). *Pirkei D'Rabbi Eliezer.* New York: Mishor Publishing.

Berman, A.L. (1974). Belief in afterlife, religion, religiosity and life-threatening experiences. *Omega, 5,* 127–135.

———, Hays, J.E. (1973). Relation between death, anxiety, belief in afterlife, and locus of control. *Journal of Consulting and Clinical Psychology, 41* (2), 318.

Bialis, L.A., & Kennedy, W.R. (1977). Effects of a death education program upon secondary school students. *Journal of Educational Research, 71,* 63–66.

Bibliotherapy Fact Sheet. (1982). Educational Resources Information Center Clearinghouse on Reading and Communication Skills: Urbana, Illinois.

Blackmore, S. (1983). *Beyond the Body.* Chicago: Academy Chicago Publishers.

Bohart, J.B., & Bergland, B.W. (1979). The impact of death and dying counseling groups on death anxiety in college students. *Death Education, 2,* 381–391.

Bond, C. (1994). Religiosity, age, gender, and death anxiety. Indiana State University: Thesis no. 1760.

Boyar, J.I. (1964). The construction and partial validation of a scale for the measurement of the fear of death. *Dissertation Abstracts (25),* 2041.

Bronson, M. (2002). Fear, death, and the fear of death. Retrieved September 5, 2004, from http://www.biblehelp.org

Burns, D., M.D. (1999). *The Feeling Good Handbook.* New York: Penguin Books.

Byrne, D. (1971). *The Attraction Paradigm*. New York: Academic Press.

Callanan, M., & Kelly, Patricia. (1997). *Final Gifts*. New York: Bantam Books.

Carington, W. (1945). *Telepathy: An Outline of its Facts, Theory, and Implications*. England: Methuen.

Carr, D. (1981). Endorphins at the approach of death. *The Lancet* (February 14, 1981): 390.

———— (1982). Pathophysiology of stress-induced limbic lobe dysfunction: A hypothesis relevant to near-death experiences. *Anabiosis: The Journal of Near-Death Studies*, 2, 75–89.

Cicirelli, Victor, G. (1997). Relationship of psychosocial and background variables to older adults' end-of-life decisions. *Psychology and Aging 12 (1)*, 72–83.

Cladder, J., M. (2000). International Board for Regression Therapy, Canastota, New York: Retrieved November 9, 2004, from http://www.ibrt.org/research.html.

Collet, L.-J., Lester, David. (1969). The fear of death and the fear of dying. *Journal of Psychology (72)*, 179–181.

Collins, G. (1970). The manipulation of human behavior. *Journal of the American Statistical Association*, 22, 8–13.

Cousins, N. (1979). *Anatomy of an Illness as Perceived by the Patient: Reflections on Healing and Regeneration*. New York: Norton.

Cozzolino, P.J., Staples, A.D., Meyers, L.S., & Samboceti, J. (2004). Greed, death, and values: From terror management to transcendence management theory. *Personality and Social Psychology Bulletin, March 2004*, 30 (3), 278–292.

DePaola, S.J., Neimeyer, R.A., Lupfer, M.B., & Fiedler, J. (1992). Death concern and attitudes toward the elderly in nursing home personnel. *Death Studies* 16, 537–555.

DePaola, S.J., Neimeyer, R.A., & Ross, S.K. (1994). Death concern and attitudes toward the elderly in nursing home personnel as a function of training. *Omega: Journal of Death and Dying*, 29, 231–248.

Dickstein, L.D. (1977–1978). Attitudes toward death, anxiety, and social desirability. *Omega* 8, 369–378.

Difede, J., & Hoffman, H. (2002). Multimedia Reviews: Innovative use of virtual reality technology in the treatment of PTSD in the aftermath of September 11. *Psychiatric Services 53* (September 2002), 1083–1085.

Dinkmeyer, D., Dinkmeyer, Don Jr., & Sperry, Len. (1987). *Adlerian Counseling and Psychotherapy, Second Edition.* Columbus, Ohio: Merrill Publishing Company.

Domalewski, S. (1999). Rape myth acceptance: Changing attitudes through the use of popular movies: Department of Psychology, Missouri Western State College. Retrieved on November 10, 2004, from http://clearinghouse.mwsc.edu. manuscripts/147.asp.

Doore, Gary, *What Survives.* Jeremy P. Tarcher Inc., Los Angeles, 1990.

Dossey, L., M.D. (1993). *Healing Words.* New York: HarperCollins.

———— (1999). *Reinventing Medicine.* San Francisco: Harper.

Durlak, J.A. (1972). Measurement of the fear of death. *Journal of Clinical Psychology* 28, 545–547.

Edwards, P. (2002). *Reincarnation: A Critical Examination.* New York: Prometheus Books.

Eppele, R. (1989). Reading material selection: K-12. Focused Access to Selected Topics (FAST) Bibliography No. 30: ERIC Clearinghouse on Reading and Communication Skills, Indiana University: Bloomington, MN.

Epting, F.R., & Neimeyer, R.A. (Eds.). (1984). *Personal Meanings of Death: Applications of Personal Construct Theory to Clinical Practice*. New York: Hemisphere/McGraw Hill.

Evans-Wentz, W.Y. (1960). *The Tibetan book of the Dead*. London: Oxford University Press.

Fang, B., & Howell, K.A. (1976). Death anxiety among graduate students. *Journal of the American College Health Association* 25, 310–313.

Fehring, R.J., Miller, J.F., & Shaw, C. (1997). Spiritual well-being, religiosity, hope, depression, and other mood states in elderly people coping with cancer. *Oncology Nursing Forum* 24, 663–671.

Filmbug. (1989). Retrieved December 27, 2004, from http://www.filmbug.com/asin/0783225881.

Finkelman, S. (2004). *More Shabbos Stories*. New York: Mesorah Publications.

Flaherty, J. (1999). *Coaching – Evoking Excellence in Others*. Massachusetts: Butterworth Heinemann.

Frankl, V., M.D. (1959). *Man's Search for Meaning*. London: Hodder and Stoughton.

———— (2004). Retrieved on November 10, 2004, from http://logotherapy.inivie.ac/at/e/logotherapy.html

Gallup, G., Jr. (1982). *Adventures in Immortality*. New York: McGraw Hill.

Garfield, C. (1979). More grist for the mill: Additional near-death research findings and discussion. *Anabiosis: The Journal of Near-Death Studies* 19, 1 (1), 5–7.

Gesser, G., Wong, P.T., & Reker, G.T. (1987–88). Death attitudes across the life span: The development and validation of the Death Attitude Profile. *Omega: Journal of Death and Dying* 18, 113–128.

Ginsburgh, Y. (2004). *Body, Mind and Soul*. Israel: Gal Einai Institute, Inc.

Goble, D. (1993). *Through the Tunnel*. Florida: S.O.U.L. Foundation.

Goldberg, C., B., & Zlotowitz, Meir (ed.). (1991). *Mourning in Halacha*. Brooklyn, New York: Mesorah Publications.

Greenberg, J., Pyszczynski, T., Solomon, S., Rosenblatt, A., Veeder, M., Kirkland, S., & Lyon, D. (1990). Evidence for terror management theory II: The effects of mortality salience on reactions to those who threaten or bolster the cultural worldview. *Journal of Personality and Social Psychology, 58,* 308–318.

Greenberg, J., Simon, L., Pyszczynski, T., Solomon, S., & Chatel, D. (1992). Terror management and tolerance: Does mortality salience always intensify negative reactions to those who threaten one's worldview? *Journal of Personality and Social Psychology, 63,* 212–220.

Greyson, B., M.D. (1981). Toward a psychological explanation of NDES. *Anabiosis: The Journal of Near-Death Studies, 1,* 88–103.

———— (1983). Near-death experiences and personal values. *American Journal of Psychiatry, 140,* 618–620.

Grinder, J., & Bandler, R. (1975). *The Structure of Magic*. Palo Alto: Science and Behavior, Inc.

Grof, S., & Halifax, Joan. (1977). *The Human Encounter with Death*. New York: E.P. Dutton.

Guthrie, S., C. (2002). Death and presentation: How mortality salience and framing affects attitudes toward welfare recipients. Paper submitted to advanced lab in social psychology: Department of Psychology, Indiana University. Retrieved December 27, 2004, from http://www.iusb.edu/~journal/2002/guthrie/html.

Halamish, Y. (1999). *Life after Death* (Hebrew). Israel: Alon Printing.

Hart, E.J. (1978–1979). The effects of death anxiety and mode of "case study" presentation on shifts of attitudes toward euthanasia. *Omega* 6, 161–170.

Hayes, J.A. & Gelso, C.J. (1993). Male counselors' discomfort with gay and HIV-infected clients. *Journal of General Psychology,* 82, 165–177.

Hayslip, B., & Stewart-Bussey, D. (1986–1987). Locus of control-levels of death anxiety. *Omega* 17, 41–50.

Hayslip, B., & Walling, M.L. (1985–1986). Impact of hospice volunteer training on death anxiety and locus of control. *Omega* 16, 243–254.

Hovland, C.I. (1959). Reconciling conflicting results derived from experimental and survey studies of attitude change. *American Psychologist* 14.

Howells, K., & Field, D. (1982). Fears of death and dying among medical students. *Social Science and Medicine* 16, 1421–1424.

Hunt, D.M., Lester, D., & Ashton, N. (1983). Fear of death, locus of control and occupation. *Psychological Reports* 53, 1022.

Iyengar, S. (1990). Framing responsibility for political issues: The case of poverty. *Political Behavior* 12, 19–40.

Jewish Tribune. (2004). *Israeli University Develops Virtual Reality Treatment Program for Victims of Terror.* Bnai Brith Canada. In Arutz 7 electronic mail news report (date unknown). Tiferet Gadi Tape Library, Jerusalem.

Jung, C. (1955). *Modern Man in Search of a Soul* (In Astor ed.). Florida: Harvest.

Juni, S., and Fischer, P.F. (1985). Religiosity and preoedipal fixation. *The Journal of Genetic Psychology* 146 (1), 27–35.

Kaplan, A. (1979). *The Bahir* (The Illumination). Maine: Weiser Books.

———— (1983). *If you were God: Three works by Aryeh Kaplan*. New York: Orthodox Union/National Conference for Synagogue Youth.

———— (1985). *The Aryeh Kaplan Reader*. New York: Mesorah Publications.

———— (1992). *Immortality, Resurrection, and the Age of the Universe*. New Jersey: Ktav.

———— (1997). *Sefer Yetzirah* (The Book of Creation). Maine: Weiser Books.

Kerenyi, C. (1967). Eleusis: Archtypal image of mother and daughter. In his series *Archtypal Images in Greek Religion*. (See Kleiman, M.)

Kienow, D.H., & Bolin, R.C. (1989–1990). Belief in afterlife: A national survey. *Omega* 20 (1), 63–74.

Kirzner, Y. (2002). *Making Sense of Suffering*. New York: Mesorah Publications.

Kleiman, M. (2004). Overcoming the fear of death. Retrieved August 10, 2004, from http://www.markarkleiman.com/archives/_/2004/03/overcoming_the_fear_of_death.php

Klemens, L. (1993). Are handicapped adolescents interested in reading fiction with handicapped characters? M.A. Thesis, Kean College.

Koestler, A. (1972). *The Roots of Coincidence*. New York: Random House.

Kook, A.Y.H., Rabbi. (1984). *Orot Hakodesh* (Hebrew). Jerusalem: Mossad Harav Kook.

Kraft, W.A., Litwin, W.J., & Barber, S.E. (1987). Religious orientation and assertiveness. *Journal of Social Psychology* 127, 93–95.

Kubler-Ross, E. (1969). *On Death and Dying.* New York: McMillan Publishing.

Kubler-Ross, E., M.D. (1982). *Working it Through.* New York: MacMillan Publishing.

——— (1991). *On Life after Death.* Berkeley: Celestial Arts Publishing.

Kubler-Ross, E., M.D. (1997). *On Children and Death.* New York: Simon and Schuster.

Kurlychek, R.T. (1976). Level of belief in afterlife and four categories of fear of death in a sample of 60+ year olds. *Psychological Reports* 38, 228.

Kurlychek, R.T. (1979). Assessment of attitudes toward death and dying – critical review of some available methods. *Omega – Journal of Death and Dying* 9.

Kurlychek, R.T., & Trepper, T.S. (1982). Accuracy of perception of attitude. *Perceptual and Motor Skills* 54, 272–274.

Kushner, H. (2001). *When Bad Things Happen to Good People.* New York: Schocken Books.

Lakin, M. (1988). *Ethical Issues in the Psychotherapies.* New York: Oxford University Press.

Lamm, M. (1969). *The Jewish Way in Death and Mourning.* New York: Jonathan David Publishers.

Lazarus, A.A. (1989). *The Practice of Multimodal Therapy.* Baltimore, MD: Johns Hopkins University Press.

Lester, D. (1967). Experimental and correlational studies of the fear of death. *Psychological Bulletin* 67, 27–36.

———. Fear of death of suicidal persons. *Psychological Reports* 20, 1077–1078.

——— (1969). Fear of death and nightmare experiences. *Psychological Reports* 25, 437–438.

——— (1970). Correlates of animism in adults. *Psychological Reports* 27, 806.

———. Religious behavior and the fear of death. *Omega* 1, 181–188.

——— (1971). Attitudes toward death and suicide in a non-disturbed population. *Psychological Reports* 29, 386.

——— (1972). Studies in death attitudes. *Psychological Reports* 30, 440.

——— (1974). The Collett-Lester fear of death scale: A manual. Pomona, New Jersey: Richard Stockton State College.

——— (1979). Preference for method of suicide and attitudes toward death in normal people. *Psychological Reports* 45, 638.

——— (1984–1985). The fear of death, sex and androgyny. *Omega* 15, 271–274.

——— (1985). Depression and fear of death in a normal group. *Psychological Reports* 56, 882.

——— (1990). The Collett-Lester fear of death scale: The original version and a revision. Pomona, New Jersey: Richard Stockton State College, Hemisphere Publishing.

Lester, D., & Blustein, J. (1980). Attitudes toward funerals. *Psychological Reports* 46, 1074.

Lester, D., & Collett, L.J. (1970). Fear of death and self-ideal discrepancy. *Archives of the Foundation of Thanatology* 2, 130.

Lester, D., & Colvin, L.M. (1977). Fear of death, alienation and self-actualization. *Psychological Reports* 41, 526.

Levine, S. (1982). *Who Dies?* New York: Doubleday.

——— (1987). *Healing into Life and Death*. New York: Doubleday.

Leviton, D., & Fretz, B. (1978–1979). Effects of death education on fear of death and attitudes toward death and life. *Omega* 9, 266–277.

Levitt, T. (1983). *The Marketing Imagination*. New York: The Free Press.

Lewis, J.W. (1993). *Fearless* – A movie masterpiece about transcendence: Retrieved December 27, 2004, from http://www.globalideasbank.org/befaft/B&A-4.html.

Lindley, J., Bryan, Sethyn, and Conley, Bob. (1981). Near-death experiences in a Pacific Northwest American population: The Evergreen study. *Anabiosis: The Journal of Near-Death Studies* 1, 104–124.

Linn, B.S., Moravec, J., & Zeppa, R. (1982). The impact of clinical experience on attitudes of junior medical students about death and dying. *Journal of Medical Education* 57, 684–691.

Linn, M.W., Linn, B.S., & Stein, S. (1983). Impact on nursing home staff of training about death and dying. *Journal of the American Medical Association* 250, 2332–2335.

Livneh, H. (1983). Death anxiety and attitudes toward disabled persons. *Psychological Reports* 53, 359–363.

——— (1985). Brief note of the structure of the Collett-Lester fear of death scale. *Psychological Reports* 56, 136–138.

———. Death attitudes and their relationship to perceptions of physically disabled persons. *Journal of Rehabilitation* 51 (1), 38–41, 80.

Locke, S., & Colligen, Daniel. (1986). *The Healer Within*. New York: E.P. Dutton.

Loo, R. (1984). Correlates of reported attitudes towards and use of seat belts. *Accident Analysis and Prevention* 16, 417–421.

———. Personality correlates of the fear of death. *Journal of Clinical Psychology* 40, 120–122.

Mangen, D.J., & Peterson, W.A. (1982). Research instruments in social gerontology (3 Vols.). *Clinical and Social Psychology,* Pr.V.1.

McDonald, R.T., & Hilgendorf, W.A. (1986). Death imagery and death anxiety. *Journal of Clinical Psychology* 42, 87–89.

McMordie, W.R. (1979). Improving measurement of death anxiety. *Psychological Reports* 44, 975–980.

Meduna, L.J. (1950). *Carbon Dioxide Therapy.* Springfield, Illinois: Charles C. Thomas.

Miller, S. (1997). *After Death – Mapping the Journey.* New York: Simon and Schuster.

Moody, R., & Perry, Paul. (1990). *Coming Back: A Psychiatrist Explores Research Findings.* New York: Bantam Books.

Moody, R., M.D. (1975). *Life After Life.* New York: Bantam Books.

———— (1977). *Reflections on Life After Life.* New York: Bantam Books.

———— (1988). *The Light Beyond.* New York: Bantam Books.

Moody, R., M.D., & Perry, Paul. (1993). *Reunions: Visionary Encounters With Departed Loved Ones.* New York: Ivy Books.

Morse, M., M.D. (1991). *Closer to the Light: Learning From Near-death Experiences of Children.* New York: Ivy Books.

Morse, M., Perry, Paul. (1992). *Transformed by the Light: The Powerful Effects of Near-Death Experiences on People's Lives.* New York: Vilard Books.

Neimeyer, R.A. (1985). Actualization, integration and fear of death. *Death Studies* 9, 235–244.

———— (1994). *Death Anxiety Handbook: Research, Instrumentation, and Application.* Washington, D.C.: Taylor and Francis.

Neimeyer, R.A., & Chapman, K.M. (1980–1981). Self-ideal discrepancy and fear of death. *Omega* 11, 233–240.

Neimeyer, R.A., & Dingemans, P.M. (1980–1981). Death orientation in the suicide intervention worker. *Omega* 11, 15–23.

Neimeyer, R.A., Bagley, K.J., & Moore, M.K. (1986). Cognitive structure and death anxiety. *Death Studies* 10, 273–288.

Nelson, T.E., & Oxley, Z.M. (1999). Issue framing effects on belief importance and opinion. *Journal of Politics* 61, 1040–1068.

Newton, M. (1994). *Journey of Souls.* St. Paul, MN: Llewellyn Publications.

Osarchuk, M., & Tatz, S.J. (1973). Effect of induced fear of death on belief in afterlife. *Journal of Personality and Social Psychology* 27.

Ouzts, D.T. (1991). The emergence of bibliotherapy as a discipline. *Reading Horizons* 31 (3), 199–206.

Paltiel, J. (2004). Meta-model and Ericsonian use of language. Paper presented at the Neuro-Linguistic Programming Lecture Series, The Refuah Institute, Jerusalem, July 15, 2004.

Pardeck, J.T., & Pardeck, Jean A. (1989). *Bibliotherapy: A Tool For Helping Preschool Children Deal With Developmental Change Related to Family Relationships.* Early Childhood Development and Care 47, 107–129.

Pardeck, J.T., & Pardeck, Jean A. (1990). Using developmental literature with collaborative groups. *Reading Improvement,* 27 (4).

Pavato, E. (1996). Review of Lakin, Martin: *Ethical Issues in the Psychotherapies* (Oxford University Press) – January 22, 1996: Retrieved December 6, 2004, from http://xaravve.trentu. ca/emma/ethical.html.

Peck, M.S. (1978). *The Road Less Traveled.* New York: Simon and Schuster.

Peterson, S.A. (1985–1986). Death anxiety and politics. *Omega* 16, 169–174.

Petty, R.E., Wegener, T.T., & Fabrigar, L.R. (1997). Attitudes and attitude change. *Annual Review of Psychology* 48.

Plutchik, R. (2000). Emotions in the practice of psychotherapy: Clinical implications of affect theories. *American Psychological Association, 139–148.*

Porter, G., & Norris, Patricia. (1986). *Why Me?* Walpole, New Hampshire: Stillpoint.

Pyszczynski, T., Greenberg, J., & Solomon, S. (1997). Why do we need what we need? A terror management perspective on the roots of human social motivation. *Psychological Inquiry* 8, 1–20.

Radin, D., & Nelson, Roger D. (1989). Consciousness-related effects in random physical systems. *Foundations of Physics* 19, 1499–1514.

Rawlings, M., M.D. (1978). *Beyond Death's Door.* New York: Bantam Books.

Ray, J.J., & Najman, J. (1974). Death anxiety and death acceptance: A preliminary approach. *Omega* 5 (4), 311–315.

Reimer, J. (1974). *Jewish Reflections on Death.* New York: Schocken Books.

Rigdon, M.A., & Epting, F.R. (1985). Reduction in death threat as a basis for optimal functioning. *Death Studies* 9, 427–448.

Ring, K. (1979). Further studies of the near-death experience. *Theta* 7, 1–3.

Ring, K. (1980). *Life at Death. New York*: William Morrow & Company.

———— (1984). *Heading Toward Omega.* New York: William Morrow & Company.

Riordan, R.J., & Wilson, Linda S. (1989). Bibliotherapy: Does it work? *Journal of Counseling and Development* 67 (9).

Robinson, P., & Wood, Keith. (1983). The threat index. *Omega* 15, 139–144.

———. The fear of death and physical illness: A personal construct approach. In *Death Ed.* Summer–Fall; 7 (2–3): 213–228. Appeared in Epting, Franz, R. (1984), *Personal Meanings of Death.* Hemisphere Publishing, p. 213–220.

Rogo, D.S. (1986). *Life After Death: The Case For Survival of Bodily Death.* Wellingborough, Northamptonshire, England: Aquarian Press.

Romm (Ed.). (1895). *Avot D'Reb Natan.* Vilna.

Rosenblatt, A., Greenberg, J., Solomon, S., Pyszczynski, T., & Lyon, D. (1989). Evidence for terror management theory I: The effects of mortality salience on reactions to those who violate or upholds cultural values. *Journal of Personality and Social Psychology* 57, 681–690.

Rosenthal, D.A., & Hunt, Brandon. (2000). Rehabilitation Counselors' experiences with client death and death anxiety. *Journal of Rehabilitation*: Retrieved on November 18, 2004, from http://findarticles.com/p/articles/mi_mo825/is_4_66/ ai_68865436.

Rossi, E., L. (1980). *Hypnotic Investigation of Psychodynamic Processes – The Collected Papers of Milton H. Erickson on Hypnosis. Volume III.* New York: Irvington Publishers, Inc.

Sabom, M., M.D. (1982). *Recollections of Death.* New York: Harper and Row.

——— (1998). *Light and Death: One Doctor's Fascinating Account of Near-death Experiences.* Michigan: Zondervan Publishing House.

Salup, B.J., & Salup, Alane. (1978). ERIC Clearinghouse on Reading and Communication Skills. Urbana, Illinois.

Salzman, M. (2001). Cultural trauma and recovery: Perspectives from terror management. *Theory, Trauma, Violence, and Abuse* 2 (2), 172–192.

Sarnoff, I., Corwin, S.M. (1959). Castration anxiety and the fear of death. *Journal of Personality* 27, 274–285.

Schmidt, H. (1976). PK effect on pre-recorded targets. *Journal of American Society for Psychical Research* 70, 267–291.

Schoenrade, P.A. (1989). When I Die: Belief in afterlife as a response to mortality. *Personality and Social Psychology Bulletin* 15 (1), 91–100.

Scholl, R.W. (2002). Attitudes and attitude change: University of Rhode Island website. Retrieved on November 9, 2004, from http://www.cba.uri.edu/scholl/notes/attitudes.htm.

Schroeder, G. (July 1, 2004). *Life After Life – The Scientific Evidence For Death as the Start of a New Phase of Life.* Paper presented at the Root and Branch Association, Jerusalem.

Schursterm, L.R., & Sechrest, L. (1973). Attitudes of registered nurses toward death in a general hospital. *International Journal of Psychiatry in Medicine* 4, 411–426.

Schwartz, G.E. (2002). *The Afterlife Experiments.* New York: Simon and Schuster.

Sergeant, D., A.J. (2003). *Window to the Light.* Australia: Imprint Books.

Servaty, H.L., Krejci, M.J., & Hayslip, B. (1996). Relationships among death anxiety, communication apprehension with the dying, and empathy in those seeking occupations as nurses and physicians. Death Studies 20, 149–161.

Simonton, O.C., Simonton, Stephanie, & Creighton, James. (1978). *Getting Well Again: A Step-by-step Self-help Guide to Overcoming Cancer For Patients and Their Families.* New York: St. Martin's.

Singh, K.D. (1998). *The Grace In Dying.* San Francisco: Harper.

Slezak, M.E. (1982). Attitudes toward euthanasia as a function of death fears and demographic variables. *Essence* 5, 191–197.

Smith, A.G. (1989). Will the real bibliotherapist please stand up? *Journal of Youth Services in Libraries* 2 (3), 241–249.

Smith, D.K., Nehemkis, A.M., & Charter, R.A. (1983–1984). Fear of death attitudes and religious conviction in the terminally ill. *International Journal of Psychiatry in Medicine* 13, 221–232.

Stephenson, I., M.D. (1987). *Children Who Remember Past Lives*. Virginia: University Press.

Stevenson, I., M.D. (1977). The evidence of man's survival after death. *Journal of Nervous and Mental Disease* 165 (3), 167–168.

Teltscher, H.O. (1993). The use of handwriting analysis in psychotherapeutic practice. *Journal of the American Society of Professional Graphologists* 3, 7–20.

Templer, D.I. (1970). Death anxiety scale: The construction and validation of a fear of death and physical illness. *Journal of General Psychology* 82, 165–177.

———, Lester, D. & Ruff, C.F. (1974). Fear of death and femininity. *Psychological Reports* 35, 530.

Testa, J.R. (1981). Group systematic desensitization and implosive therapy for death anxiety. *Psychological Reports* 48, 376–378.

Thomas, L. (1977). Notes of a biology-watcher: Facts of Life. *New England Journal of Medicine* 296 (25): 1462–1464.

Thorson, J.A., & Powell, F.C. (1984, November). Revision and factor analysis of a death anxiety scale. Paper presented at the 37ᵗʰ annual meeting of the Gerontological Society, San Antonio, TX.

Thorson, J.A., & Powell, F.C. (1988). Elements of death, anxiety, and meanings of death. *Journal of Clinical Psychology* 44 (5), 691–701.

Thorson, J.A., & Powell, F.C. (1994). *A revised death anxiety scale.* In R.A. Neimeyer (Ed.), Death Anxiety Handbook: Research, Instrumentation, and Application (31–43). Washington, D.C.: Taylor and Francis.

Tucazinsky, Rabbi Y.M. (1949). *The Bridge of Life* (Translated from Hebrew by Rabbi N.A. Tucazinsky). Jerusalem: Moznaim Publishing.

Twelker, Paul A. (2004). The relationship between death anxiety, sex and age. Retrieved on January 3, 2005, from: http://www.tiu.edu/psychology/deathanxiety.htm.

Twemlow, S., Gabbard, Glen, and Jones, Fowler. (1981). Do near-death experiences occur only near death? *Journal of Nervous and Mental Disease* 169, 374–377.

van Lommel, P., van Wees, Ruud, Meyers, Vincent, & Elfferich, Ingrid. (2001). Near-death experience in survivors of cardiac arrest: a prospective study in the Netherlands. *The Lancet* 358 (9298), 2039–2045.

Vargo, M.E. (1980). Relationship between the Templer death anxiety scale and the Collett-Lester fear of death scale. *Psychological Reports* 46, 561–562.

Vargo, M.E., & Batsel, W.M. (1984). The reduction of death anxiety. *British Journal of Medical Psychology* 57, 334–337.

Vital, C., HaRav. (1684 C.E.). *The Book of Incarnations* (Heb. Sefer HaGilgulim): Chapters 64, 69.

Vorst, Y. (1991). *Why? Reflections on the Loss of a Loved One.* Jerusalem: Feldheim Publishing.

Walle, A., H. (2004). *Terror Management: A Model of International Interaction.* Paper presented at the Nabsite Conference, Las Vegas, Nevada.

Weiss, B., M.D. (1988). *Many Lives, Many Masters*. New York: Simon & Schuster.

Wexelman, D.M. (1999). *Jewish Concept of Reincarnation and Creation: Based on the Writings of Rabbi Chaim Vital*. Maryland: Rowman and Littlefield Publishers.

White, R. (1989). Bibliotherapy and the reluctant student: Educational Resources Information Center Clearinghouse on Reading and Communication Skills, Indiana University: Bloomington, MN.

Yalom, I., M.D. (2000). *Love's Executioner and Other Tales of Psychotherapy*. New York: Perennial Classics.

Yalom, I., M.D. (2000). *Mama and the Meaning of Life*. New York: HarperCollins Publishers.

Yellinek, A. (1967). *Sefer Bet Midrash Cheder Rishon*. Third Edition. Jerusalem.

Zohar Chadash 33a.

Zohar 1:186b.

About the Author

Dr. Bernie D. Kastner completed his undergraduate studies at Yeshiva University and his graduate work in public health at Columbia University. He went on to become certified as a handwriting expert and has incorporated this specialized discipline into his counseling work. After completing advanced training in counseling at The William Glasser Institute, he became certified as a reality therapist. Dr. Kastner's research has focused on new therapeutic approaches in dealing with death anxiety, end-of-life issues, and bereavement with particular emphasis on personal growth and healing. Dr. Kastner is currently in private practice as a psychotherapist in Jerusalem where he counsels individuals, families, educators, and providers of care. Dr. Kastner can be reached at BDK15@columbia.edu.